ENDORSEMENTS:

"Spiritual authority is not determined by who submits to you, but rather to whom you are submitted". In nearly forty years as a believer in Yeshua (Jesus) I don't know that I have ever met another believer who has not been injured in some way due to the misuse of authority. In this studied approach, Asher helps us to understand the 'how and why' of spiritual and delegated authority, and not just the 'what'. Asher's extensive background as a disciplined student of the Word of God, and his passion as a pioneer in the Messianic Jewish movement in the U.S. and Israel have made him a trusted teacher and pastor internationally…and the spiritual authority to whom I am submitted!

- PAUL WILBUR, Executive Director, International Messianic Jewish Alliance and Pastor of Jewish Ministries, Celebration Church

Asher Intrater, a Messianic apostle to believers in Israel, brings balance and clarity as he lays out the scriptural foundation for all authority which has been given to us by God. Asher's fresh revelation and deep understanding of scripture from a Jewish mindset will challenge old ways of thinking. You will find yourself being catapulted to new heights as you awaken to the true authority available to believers. Be blessed as you read and meditate on the truths in *All Authority*.

- JANE HANSEN HOYT, President, Aglow International

I have greatly appreciated Asher's teaching for many years. I find rich insight and heart felt inspirations. This book is no exception. There is a great need in the body of Christ to understand Jesus' authority that is manifest directly and delegated through people. It is essential in seeing His Kingdom established on earth. Asher's ability to state profound truths in a simple way is a great gift to so many.

- MIKE BICKLE, Founder and Director, International House of Prayer, Kansas City

My friend and colleague of almost 40 years, Asher Intrater has written an important and poignant book on authority. It is profound, clear and balanced. It is desperately needed.

- DR. DANIEL C. JUSTER, Director and Co-Founder, Tikkun International

I'm blown away by the breadth and depth of Asher's distilled *magnum opus*. This collection of insights and brilliantly interwoven references contains a panoramic view yet with personal application. I'm stunned, shaking my head--can't contain all that he's injected into an admirably compact work. Provocative & Relevant.

- EITAN SHISHKOFF, Founder & Director, Tents of Mercy and Co-Founder of Tikkun International

ALL AUTHORITY

BIBLICAL PRINCIPLES OF SPIRITUAL AND DELEGATED AUTHORITY

ASHER INTRATER

All Authority: Biblical Principles of Spiritual and Delegated Authority

Published By:
Revive Israel Media
206 East 4th Street
Frederick, MD 21701
www.reviveisrael.org

Cover design and interior layout by www.PearCreative.ca

ISBN 978-1-941941-75-1

All translations in this book are the author's. Translations from the Hebrew Scriptures are direct from the original Hebrew. Translations of the New Covenant are a reconstruction adapted from the Modern Hebrew Translation (The Bible Society in Israel). Hebrew text translations are occasionally compared to the New King James Version, © Thomas Nelson Publishers.

TABLE OF CONTENTS

FOREWORD

I can think of no topic more misunderstood yet more important than spiritual authority. Generally speaking Bible teachers tend to emphasize just one perspective in dealing with authority; and therefore, by the very nature of the teaching, there is imbalance and extremism.

The subject is so vast that it cannot be dealt with fully in just one book. This book is an attempt to summarize the different aspects of spiritual and delegated authority in a balanced and practical way. The material in the main sections of the book is very condensed. I would suggest that not more than one chapter be read on any given day.

The book is meant to change the heart of the reader to have more healthy attitudes concerning authority. The principles described here were derived by decades of real-life experiences and are meant to be applied in real relationships in everyday life.

The purpose of authority is to bring blessing. May you be blessed by studying this training and instruction manual!

From my heart to yours,

אשר אינטרטר

Asher Intrater

PART ONE:
FOUNDATIONS OF AUTHORITY

CHAPTER ONE
ATTITUDES TOWARD AUTHORITY

Quite frankly, my personal background as a young adult did not include a positive attitude toward authority at all.

In school growing up, I found myself in a surprising number of positions of authority among my peers. I was president of the senior class at Whitman High School in Bethesda, Maryland (in fact 3 out of 4 years from 9th to 12th grade); president of confirmation class at Bethel Synagogue; and president of a three-state *Civitan* service organization. Then I was accepted to Harvard College.

At that point, which should have been the beginning of a successful and prosperous career, my world view began to disintegrate. I could not understand why I existed or where I was going. I began to "search for spiritual truth," which involved discarding many socially acceptable standards.

I studied philosophy for a while at Harvard, and became an "existential nihilist" (which means that we just "exist" and there is no meaning to our existence; "Nihilo" is "nothing" in Latin). To demonstrate my philosophical position, I once sat on the floor of an elevator on campus and when someone would enter the elevator and ask me where I was going, I would say, "What difference does it make?"

From there I went on to all kinds of experiences in my search for spiritual truth. These included psychology, folklore, mythology, literature, Buddhism, Hinduism, drugs, immorality, and a variety of other misguided adventures. The only thing I would not consider, of course, was Jesus. (After all, I'm Jewish and a college graduate, etc.)

Those years of the early and mid- 1970's were marked by a breakdown of authority throughout the Western world. The Watergate scandal, the Vietnam War, drugs, rock concerts, counter culture demonstrations, women's liberation, the sexual "revolution" and much more, turned everyone's values "upside-down."

A parallel experience was happening with the youth in Israel. After the 1967 "Six-day War" victory, the Israeli public thought they were invincible. In the euphoria and self-delusion, they were unprepared for the massive attack in the "Yom Kippur War" of 1973. The nation faced the possibility of sudden and total annihilation.

Israeli youth, because of the Yom Kippur War, like American youth because of the Vietnam War, faced a similar dissolution of values and moral assumptions which led them into a parallel and bizarre reevaluation of their most basic world views.

One of the prominent themes of the late 1960's and 70's was the image of the "rebel hero." Che Guevara with his fist raised, militant Black Muslims with their fists raised, and rock stars with their middle finger raised were all images of a new kind of hero. Rebellion in and of itself was glorified as the highest level of ethical standards.

In the West, political propaganda, sensual entertainment and strange academic theories brain-washed our generation that rebellion was an expression of moral conscience, and that all forms of authority were evil. In China, Mao and the Cultural Revolution encouraged an entire generation of Chinese youth to rebel against every form of traditional authority in the name of a utopian, communist theory.

I developed a philosophy that life is simply an accumulation of meaningless experiences, and the only reasonable response is to try every possible experience, whether good or bad. Taste every food, travel to every country, read every book, play every game, sin every sin, and so on.

Then someone challenged me to read the New Testament. I was not at all interested and totally convinced that it could have no truth in it. Yet to be consistent with my personal philosophy, I had to "check it out." The big surprise was that the one thing I was not willing to consider turned out to be the one person who had answers to life.

My search for spiritual truth came to a wonderful climax in the one who is "the way, the truth and the life" (**John 14:6**). After the initial joy of revelation of the love of God, I was met with another dilemma. God was not calling me to just believe in him as a philosophy, but to follow him with my whole life.

How could I follow Jesus? This was against every social, family, philosophical, educational, and religious code I had been brought up with. I would have to go "against" everything. In a strange way, this was the ultimate act of moral rebellion. Even if the whole world is against me, if Jesus is the truth, then I will follow him, no matter what will happen.

To follow Yeshua (Jesus) for me was an act of self-denial and rebellion against everything I had known. It was a total reversal of values. The wheel had gone around 360 degrees. Rebellion had become submission; and submission had become rebellion. Paradoxically, by way of rebellion against all authority, I had come face to face with the one who claimed to be the source of "all authority."

At the end of the gospel of Matthew, Yeshua made an amazing statement concerning authority.

Matthew 28:18

All authority has been given to me in heaven and on earth...

If this was true, then I needed to reexamine every thought I had ever had about authority. If "all authority" is from him, then "all" my thoughts about authority were wrong. There was nothing to do but submit. This is a real revolution – a revolution concerning rebellion, and a revolution concerning authority.

These words from Matthew were a summary of Yeshua's last teaching on earth before He ascended into heaven. In some ways, this is a summary statement of all Yeshua did on earth from the time he was born until the time he was raised from the dead.

Part of his mission to earth was to recover and repair the evils that had been done in the name of authority. As the only citizen of both heaven and earth, he was the only one who could unite the two spheres of authority, above and below (See Supplement 1: Heaven and Earth).

This statement that he has all authority in heaven and earth represents a new rank or position. By means of his death and resurrection, Yeshua came into a new standing of spiritual authority that had never existed before. His obedience on the cross and the power of the resurrection acquired a dimension of authority hitherto unknown.

After Yeshua was raised from the dead, he taught his disciples for 40 days concerning the kingdom of God (**Acts 1:3**). That kingdom was his kingdom, the kingdom of the Messiah, the kingdom of Israel (**Acts 1:6**), in which God's will would be done on earth as it is in heaven (**Matthew 6:10**).

A kingdom is an area in which a king has authority. It is the area of his dominion. A king"dom" is a king's "dominion." Yeshua is declaring that his dominion as king now includes both heaven and earth. This authority is unprecedented and all-inclusive.

The declaration of Yeshua's authority is not only a summary of his life's work and of his 40-day "post-resurrection" teaching, it is also the basis for sending his disciples out to continue his mission. It is the basis for the *Great Commission*:

Matthew 28:18-19

All authority has been given to me in heaven and on earth. Go therefore and make disciples of all nations...

Yeshua came to earth on a mission to seek and save the lost (**Luke 19:10; I Timothy 1:15**); to demonstrate the love of God (**Romans 5:8; I John 4:9**); to destroy the works of the devil (**I John 3:8**); and to give us an example of servanthood and obedience (**Matthew 20:28; Philippians 2:5-8**). However, he also came to receive kingdom authority for himself (**Luke 19:12; John 18:37; Philippians 2:9-10**).

After his resurrection and before his final ascension, he gave his disciples instructions to continue his mission. He came from heaven to earth with a mission; they were to extend that mission to all the nations. His mission became their commission.

Paul's version of the great commission emphasizes righteousness by faith (**Romans 1:17**); Peter emphasizes faith and miracles (**Mark 16:15-18**); and Luke emphasizes forgiveness and the baptism of the Holy Spirit (**Luke 24:49; Acts 1:4-5**). However Matthew's version emphasizes authority and discipleship.

Yeshua said that "all authority" was given to him. That statement demands a total reevaluation about how we view authority. My hope is that this booklet might serve as a discipleship guide to explore and develop right attitudes toward authority.

QUESTIONS FOR REFLECTION:

What is Yeshua's dominion? That is, what does he have authority over?

What experiences in your life have influenced your view of authority?

How have those experiences affected your view of authority? List good and bad effects.

CHAPTER TWO
HEALING FROM ABUSE

All authority in heaven and earth comes from God through Yeshua. The Bible has much to say about authority, although the word authority is not mentioned very often. The Bible uses many terms to express authority, such as *king, kingdom, throne, keys, scepter, principality, name, Messiah, Lord, Adonai, commandments* and *Father*.

Let's start with the image of Father. Yeshua revealed to us the full nature of God as a loving Father.

John 17:25

O righteous Father, the world has not known you, but I have known you… and I have declared to them your name, and will declare it, that the love with which you loved me may be in them.

The letters of the alphabet in Hebrew have numerical values. Aleph is 1. Bet is 2. The name for Father is Ab, or for Daddy is Abba: אבא Aleph-Bet-Aleph. This is the first possible word numerically that can be formed: 1-2 or 1-2-1. In the Hebrew interplay on numbers and letters, we can understand that in the biblical language, "Abba" is the foundational numerical value for every other word or name.

God is Father; God is Abba.

Let us define Father – "father" is the combination of two elements: love and authority.

Without love, you have a boss. Without authority you have a boyfriend. When you put love and authority together, you have the image of a father. Therefore the biblical concept of authority is essentially connected to love. Biblical authority is loving authority. Love and authority go together. The image of God as father joins the concepts of love and authority inseparably into one.

For example, part of a father's job is to protect his daughter from sexual immorality until the day he transfers her protection into the hands of a loving husband. The world of modern entertainment has despised the image of a father, at the same time it has glamorized the image of sexual relations outside of marriage.

Sexual immorality depends on weakening the authority of the father. In modern entertainment it is rare to find the image of a dad who is wise, kind, loving, moral, strong and authoritative. At the same time the images of "fun" and excitement in sexual relations are all pictured as outside of marriage. This is not a coincidence.

I thank God that my own dad was a good model for me of the balance between love and authority. On the one hand, he was a tough lawyer in the Washington, D. C. legal world. On the other hand, he always demonstrated to me affection and tenderness.

Until the day he went to be with the Lord, his eyes would well up with tears whenever he saw me. Yet when we were young, my brother and I always feared his authority.

Perhaps because of my dad, it is not very difficult for me to see authority and love combined. There is no contradiction. I have a mental association of love-dad-authority that goes together. Therefore perhaps as well, the idea of God as a Father and as a loving authority seems obvious. (When I first believed in Yeshua, I came back and told my dad, "I have two fathers now." He had no problem understanding that I was referring to him as my dad and also to God our Father.)

Yet, how can people who have had a negative experience with their own fathers develop a right attitude toward authority? Many fathers were abusive physically, verbally, emotionally, even sexually. Many fathers abandoned their families or were alcoholics, workaholics or addicted to gambling. Many were silent, cold, and unexpressive. Some were mentally unstable, dysfunctional and psychologically imbalanced. Others left their wives and children to be with a younger woman.

It may be a challenge for someone coming from a background of an abusive or abdicating father to have a good relationship with God, who is a "heavenly Father." What does that terminology convey to them? What mental pictures must they overcome to believe that God loves them, can be trusted, and will never leave them?

What about people who have been abused or abandoned by other authority figures – an employer, a teacher, a pastor, a rabbi, a military commander, a police officer, a husband?

When my wife came to the Lord, also in the 1970's, she served as the personal secretary of the leader of a large network of Christian communities, mostly young people. They were intensely and zealously devoted to discipleship, prayer, Bible study, evangelism, and serving the poor. In the early days it was ideal.

As time went on, the leader became somewhat abusive and manipulative, even calling himself the new "Elijah." The group took on cultish and oppressive tendencies. Finally my wife had to flee the group. When we met, it took some time for her to go through a healing process to overcome that traumatic experience.

Unfortunately, over the years, we have seen many pastors behave in manipulative and abusive ways. For a person to be a dominant leader, he must have charismatic, gifted and often godly aspects to his personality. If not, no one would follow him. Therefore, it is difficult for people who have been under manipulative and abusive leadership to recover from the hurts and confusion involved.

Before one can learn to relate properly to godly authority, he or she must be healed of improper relations with ungodly authority. We want a true "abba," not abuse or abandonment. Discipleship is learning to respond correctly to Yeshua's authority. The first step is to be healed from painful experiences with incorrect authority.

Let us remember that human fathers, and all other human authorities, are always both <u>imperfect</u> and <u>temporary.</u>

Hebrews 12:9-10

> **We had human fathers who corrected us, and we paid them respect. Shall we not much more readily be in subjection to the Father of spirits and live? They chastened us for a few days as seemed best to them, but He for our benefit...**

In prayer I once saw a picture in my heart of a large system of pipes, like a plumbing installation or cathedral organ, between heaven and earth. I interpreted this picture to be an image of God's manifold system of authority flowing down toward us. The system was correct but it was being "manned" by imperfect, even sinful, human beings.

The source was good and the system was good, but the human agents involved were often bad. Discerning the difference between the divine source and the human agents is essential to set us free from bad past experiences with authority and to enable us to respond correctly to authority in the future.

Relationships between parents and children are mentioned two times in the Ten Commandments. Both involve spiritual transfer from the parents to the children; one is bad and one is good.

Deuteronomy 5:9

… visiting the sins of the parents upon the children.

The influence of the parents' sinful behavior upon the children is obviously negative, while the benefits of the children honoring their parents are many:

Deuteronomy 5:16

Honor your father and your mother that your days might be long and in order that it might be well with you upon the earth.

The negative spiritual transfer from parents to children is called a "curse." The positive spiritual transfer is a "blessing." If we find ourselves in a curse situation, we need to break that negative transfer, forgive our parents, and turn to the blessings.

[**Note:** The case of Noah shows us the complexity of parental authority, blessing and cursing. In general, Noah was a righteous man (**Genesis 6:9**). He was what we might call today a "believer."

In fact he was sort of in the ministry, "a preacher of righteousness" (**II Peter 2:5**).

Yet Noah was a "minister," who had a slight problem with alcohol. Once he got totally drunk and embarrassed himself in a disgusting way in front of his family (**Genesis 9:21**). So who is at fault at this point? So far, his three boys have done nothing. This is a crisis. They don't know what to do? In such a situation, who would want to discuss issues of righteousness, faith, parental authority, the ministry, spiritual inheritance?

One of his sons (Shem) takes an active role to protect his honor and cover up the shameful and sinful situation. The second son (Yapheth) is somewhat passive but helps out his brother. The third son (Ham) mocks and laughs at his father. What we might not notice is that in a human psychological view, Ham certainly had grounds to disrespect his father since his father acted in a dishonorable manner.

Despite the awkwardness and ugliness of the situation, God rewarded Shem for honoring his father despite his father's sin. Shem became the father of the "chosen" lineage (**Genesis 11:10**). Yapheth was also blessed, but less. Ham brought upon himself dishonor for having dishonored his father – even though his father had sinned. Despite Noah's sin, the blessing came to Shem and the curse fell to Ham.]

Part of a successful transition from childhood to adulthood is to perceive which influences from our parents were positive and which were negative. We reject the negative and receive the positive. We break the curse and restore the blessing. This principle holds true for all other kinds of authority figures in our lives.

God desires to heal us of hurtful experiences from our parents or other authority figures. God will take us in His arms to heal us on the inside with a greater measure of grace and blessing than the degree to which our parents, pastors and employers have misused us (Romans 5:20-21).

Psalm 27:10

When my father and my mother forsake me, then YHVH will gather me up.

Psalm 103:13

As a father has compassion on his children, so will YHVH have compassion on those who revere Him.

Turning to God to receive inner healing from abusive and improper authority in our lives is the first step to blessing. This healing must take place deep within our souls. Only God's perfect fathering love and affection can heal us of the hurts from wrong authority.

Unfortunately, here in Israel today, there is rampant sexual immorality in the schools and teenage social life. Many of the young people, particularly girls, but also some of the boys, experience some sort of sexual abuse from authority figures before they reach adulthood. The same is true, of course, for many other nations of the world.

Since the economic situation is so difficult, the style of authority of the employers can be extremely harsh. That economic hardship also causes pressure within the family, and the parents are often frustrated and angry. Many people have suffered abusive relationships both at home and at the work place from bosses. This harshness leaves deep emotional wounding.

Because of the constant threat of war, jihad and terrorism, the army plays a central role in our society. All of the teenagers are drafted immediately after high school. While we are extremely grateful for our defense forces, and while the IDF may very well be the most moral army in the world, military life can be very harsh. The young commanders have hardly reached the age of 20 and don't know how to exercise authority in a balanced way. Many of the new soldiers suffer manipulative and abusive relationships from their officers.

These factors and many more create a situation in which the majority of people in Israel feel they have suffered abuse from an authority figure. The same likely holds true for other countries and societies in the world today. *(If you are reading this now, and feel emotional and psychological pain from abusive authority relationships, please know that is certainly NOT the will of God.)*

God desires to heal you of abusive authority. Only God's love as an affectionate Father can heal you. The anointing of the Holy Spirit can bring healing to the "broken hearted" (**Isaiah 61:1-3**). This was a primary part of Yeshua's mission in this world: to show us right loving authority and to heal the broken hearted.

Please turn to God as your loving heavenly Father for healing in your soul and spirit, and seek those who can give you wise counsel and anointed prayer concerning any area of abuse from authority figures. The future of your spiritual life and emotional well-being is dependent on this crucial issue.

QUESTIONS FOR REFLECTION:

Is it easy for you to picture God as a loving Father? Why or why not?

Have you suffered abuse at the hands of a spiritual authority in your life?

Have you asked the Lord to help you forgive those figures so that you can rightly align yourself with His authority in your life?

CHAPTER THREE
ROOTS OF REBELLION

If we are willing to reexamine our attitude toward authority, and be healed of abusive experiences with authority, we can then look at the root of rebellion in our own lives.

The Bible tells us that God created two kinds of beings in his own image: angels and humans. All of the angels were originally good. One of the highest angels was called *Lucifer (Hillel ben Shachar)*, but he became filled with pride and jealousy, and thus turned into *Satan*, meaning *enemy*. (An image of the "fall of Lucifer" may be seen in the descriptions of the "king" of Babylon in Isaiah 14:12-17, and the "king" of Tyre in Ezekiel 28:12-19.) He led part of the angels to turn to evil. *Demons* are simply those angels who followed Satan and turned bad.

Satan wanted to become God and take God's glory. However, he could not find a way to do so. When God made Adam in His own image, it seems that Satan became extremely offended. Man was inferior to Satan, less intelligent, less glorious, and less powerful. Yet God gave man dominion over all the earth. He made man essentially to be a "delegated god" over this planet (Psalm 8).

Not only that, but God created for man a beautiful helper called woman. Neither men nor angels had seen such a beautiful creature. Satan wanted to steal Adam's authority on this planet and become the god of this world (**John 12:31, 14:30, 16:11, II Corinthians 4:4, Ephesians 2:2**). The evil angels lusted after the human women as well (**Genesis 6:4**).

So Satan tempted the woman, who in turn persuaded Adam. They both succumbed to Satan's influence and fell from their position of authority and glory. They allowed Satan to steal their authority on this planet. From that moment on, satanic spirits dominated affairs in this world through pride, lust, lies, jealousy and anger. Satan had usurped all the authority that had originally been given to Adam (**Luke 4:6**).

Since God had transferred authority on planet earth to Adam (**Psalm 115:16**), and since human beings were sinning willfully and yielding their authority to Satan, God could not immediately take the planet back by force. Yet God had a plan in which a perfect human would come one day from the seed of the woman and an offspring of Adam, who would reverse Satan's deception and win the human race and planet earth back for God (**Genesis 3:15**). We call this the "plan of redemption."

Adam and Eve had two sons at the beginning. *Hevel* (Abel) was good; *Kayin* (Cain) was evil. It would have seemed obvious that Abel was the seed who was destined to defeat the serpent. So Satan influenced Cain by anger and jealousy to murder Abel (**John 8:44, I John 3:8**). Satan's plan seemed unbeatable. He could tempt most human beings. If there was one potentially righteous, he would have one of the evil humans murder him. (Notice that the serpent of **Genesis 3** is clearly identified as Satan in **Revelation 20:2**.)

Thank God, one day, Yeshua would be born into the earth as the perfect son of Adam and recover Adam's lost authority. In the meantime, world society has been steeped in evil (**I John 5:19**). When we look at the root of evil from the book of Genesis, we find 4 different levels:

1. **Adam** – <u>Abdicated</u> his authority by unbelief. He should have told Eve not to eat the fruit and demand the snake to get out of the garden. God held Adam responsible, because He had delegated to Adam the authority.

2. **Eve** – Deceived by simple lusts and lies. She <u>sinned</u>. Her sin brought Adam's downfall as well, caused them to lose their glory, and allowed death to enter the world.

3. **Cain** – Committed a <u>criminal</u> act of murder. This was a worse level of wrong-doing than Eve. Eve did not intend to hurt anyone, she just sinned. Cain gave himself to Satan with the intention of destroying Abel.

4. **Satan** – Desired a total <u>rebellion</u> against God. Even Cain, acting out of his anger, did not intend to overthrow God and usurp God's authority. Perhaps Cain's criminal act could be forgiven, but Satan's rebellion against God is not possible to repair or redeem.

Let's simplify these 4 levels of evil. Each level is worse than the previous.

1. **Passivity: Abdication of authority**

2. **Sin: Yielding to selfishness**

3. **Crime: Hurting others**

4. **Rebellion: Intentionally overthrowing God's authority**

Adam abdicated; Eve sinned; Cain committed a crime; Satan rebelled against God. Eve's sin was worse than Adam's. Cain's crime was worse than Eve's. Satan's rebellion was worse than Cain's.

When seen from the perspective and logic of God, rebellion is the worst of all evils. The root of all human sin is Satan's rebellion. Satanic rebellion is the worst of all evils. Satan's rebellion is the spiritual source of human rebellion. When humans rebel, we do not realize how evil it is, or how much it is inspired by this demonic influence.

Unfortunately, we have all participated in this spirit and this satanic root of rebellion.

Ephesians 2:2-3

Once you walked in the age of this world, according to the prince who has the power of the air, the spirit who now works in the sons of rebellion, among whom we also all once conducted ourselves in the lusts of our flesh… and were by nature children of wrath, just as the others.

We do not tend to think that we are in demonic opposition to God. We just want our lusts, pride, honor, comforts and desires fulfilled. We don't realize that what seems to be "normal" selfishness, sinfulness and carnality, is actually sweeping us along in a stream to cooperate with demonic spirits in rebellion against God.

Let's take the example of Herodias' daughter. King Herod had taken his brother's wife, Herodias. John the Baptist had publicly rebuked them for this sin. At his birthday party, Herod had Herodias' daughter dance for him. He was excited at her sensual dance and promised her any reward. Prompted by her mother Herodias, she requested to have John beheaded (and perhaps the daughter in her brazenness added the detail of bringing his head on a platter). Now Herod did not really want to go along with this criminal act, but yielded to the peer pressure around him (**Matthew 14:1-11, Mark 6:17-29**).

Let's look at the levels of evil.

1. **Herod** - Like Adam, he had yielded to Herodias and abdicated his authority.

2. **Herodias' daughter** – Like Eve, she did not understand everything that was happening. She was just enjoying the attention of being the most desired and sensual dancer in the nation, enjoying the lusts of this world and its pleasure.

3. **Herodias** – Like Cain, she wanted to kill John the Baptist for having humiliated her. While her daughter sinned, Herodias committed murder.

4. **Jezebel** – Behind these sins major demonic spirits were at work, which were fighting against John because he was proclaiming the coming of the Messiah who would destroy the works of Satan. We refer to the demonic spirits who work in this fashion as *Jezebel* (see below).

Again we see the same 4 levels.

1. **Abdication**

2. **Sin**

3. **Crime**

4. **Satanic rebellion**

Spirits of Jezebel in our society deceive people into thinking that sexual immorality, lesbianism and homosexuality are good; that all male authority is evil; that throwing off the "yoke" of traditional family and marital values is good; and that new-age spiritism is good, while faith in God is bad. Young women today, like Herodias' daughter, think they are just expressing their own creativity, sensuality and independence. They don't realize how they are being duped by demonic spirits.

[While Queen Jezebel, the wife of Ahab, was a human being and a specific historical figure, her name became a prototype for an evil spirit that influences women to act in a similar way (**I Kings 21:25, Rev. 2:20**). A parallel spirit in men is called *Balaam*, who is also a specific historical figure as well as a spiritual prototype (**Numbers 31:16, Rev. 2:14**).]

Our seemingly normal human acts of unbelief, cowardice, lust and even crime are causing us to be puppets in the hands of Satan in his rebellion against God and his usurping us of our own glory, righteousness and authority. Little do people realize when they rebel how much they are actually submitting to and being deceived by demonic spirits (**Eph. 2:2-3**).

I Samuel 15:23

For rebellion is as the sin of witchcraft.

We are not normally aware of the spiritual power behind rebellion. Witchcraft will eventually lead to rebellion, and rebellion is fueled by evil spirits. What sometimes seems like just doing "our own thing" can be a deception in which we are blinded to the huge amounts of spiritual damage taking place.

This should make us want to wake up immediately and repent. We want to "vomit" out of ourselves all satanic spirits and roots of rebellion. Let us take a moment right now to repent of our sins and remove all demonic deception and rebellion at the deepest levels of our hearts.

QUESTIONS FOR REFLECTION

What is the spiritual origin of evil in the human race?

What are the four different levels of evil and sin?

How does sin and rebellion deceive us?

What is the connection between rebellion and witchcraft?

CHAPTER 4
OBEDIENCE AND SALVATION

If the root of our problem with authority goes all the way back to the first sin of Adam and the rebellion of Satan, then the solution to the problem must go all the way back to this root as well. Adam and Eve sinned at the tree of the knowledge of good and evil; it was there as well that the serpent Satan usurped their authority and worked his rebellion against God.

The solution goes to the root of the problem: the Tree. There is a parallel between the cross of Yeshua and the tree of Eden. The crucifixion is a substitute or atonement for the sin of Adam at the tree of the knowledge of good and evil. The word for *wood* and *tree* are the same in Hebrew: **Etz** עץ. The wood of the cross and the wood of the tree are the same. (Therefore the words *tree* and *wood* stand out as symbolic references to the cross in a reading of the Hebrew text of the Law and Prophets.)

The tree of the cross replaced the tree of knowledge. The first-century apostles and disciples well knew that the death penalty of the Torah required the criminal to be "hanged on a tree"

(**Deuteronomy 21:22**). They did not yet have a reference in their Hebraic thought for the Roman punishment of crucifixion. Therefore they often referred to the cross as the "tree":

Acts 5:30

You killed Yeshua by hanging him on the <u>tree</u>.

Acts 10:39

They killed him by hanging on a <u>tree</u>.

Acts 13:29

They took him down from the <u>tree</u> and placed him in a grave.

The crucifixion at the tree of the cross was a reversal of the sin at the tree of knowledge. The cross is like a dentist's drill doing root canal surgery all the way to the root of Adam's sin and Satan's rebellion.

Therefore, to be set free of sin and rebellion and to be restored to our pre-destined place of authority, we must embrace the tree of the cross. Yeshua's crucifixion works inside of our hearts to reverse the work of Adam's sin and Satan's rebellion. One tree replaces the other. We activate Yeshua's crucifixion in our hearts by faith and obedience.

As Adam disobeyed at the tree, Yeshua obeyed at the tree. If we identify in our own hearts with Yeshua's obedience unto death, then the power of his obedience changes our hearts to be like his. We are to have the same attitude that Yeshua had.

Philippians 2:5

Let the same attitude be in you as it was in Messiah Yeshua.

And what was that attitude? – To be willing to obey and submit even unto death.

Philippians 2:8

He humbled himself and became obedient to death, even death on the cross.

His obedience replaces Adam's disobedience. Yeshua changes our hearts from being disobedient like Adam's to being obedient like His. In fact, Yeshua had to learn obedience even as a teenager by submitting to His parents Joseph and Miriam's authority (**Luke 2:51**). He continued to learn obedience by going through suffering during His adult years (**Hebrews 5:8**).

We identify and become unified with Him on the tree of the cross. We express that union-identification with Yeshua through immersion in water (baptism).

Romans 6:4-6

We were buried with him through immersion into death… just so we also walk in newness of life. If we have been united together in the likeness of his death…

Our old man was crucified with him… that we should no longer be slaves of sin.

The cross changes our innermost being from one like Adam's to one like Yeshua's. When a person passes through the water of immersion, his heart should be changed forevermore from disobedience to obedience, from rebellion to submission.

The miracle of salvation includes within it the commitment to obey (**Romans 1:5; 6:16; 16:26**). The word *Messiah* also means *King*. If we receive Yeshua as King Messiah, we enter into His kingdom. Therefore we must agree to obey the rules of His kingdom. When someone becomes a citizen of a new country, he agrees to obey the laws of that nation as part of the process of citizenship.

Some ask the question if it is possible to receive Yeshua as savior without receiving him as lord. I do not believe so. The most basic confession of salvation is in fact a profession that one is receiving Yeshua as lord.

Romans 10:9

If you confess with your mouth that Yeshua is Lord…, you will be saved.

The word here for Lord is the Greek *Kurios.* This word has several meanings including lord as authority and lord as *Adonai-YHVH*. (See Supplement 2: Kurios.) To proclaim that someone is your lord is to commit yourself to submit to that person's authority and to obey that person's will. To remove the aspect of authority from the message of salvation is to rob it of much of its meaning.

Thank God, little by little, we are seeing more people in Israel believe in Yeshua as Messiah. In prayer for salvation, we ask new believers to declare that they believe in Yeshua's death for forgiveness of sins and in His resurrection for eternal life. We then continue with the commitment to follow after Yeshua and obey Him all the days of their life. This makes the salvation prayer much clearer and easier to understand.

The word "lord" means authority. The confession that Yeshua is Lord is a covenant declaration to accept His authority. It demands lifetime commitment just as the covenant vows of a man and a woman under the marriage canopy. As rebellion against God's authority through Satan brought eternal damnation, so does submission to God's authority through Yeshua bring eternal salvation. It's that logical and simple.

The declaration that Yeshua is Lord, when intended with true heart commitment, places us in right order towards God's authority. The declaration that Yeshua is Lord is found three times in the New Covenant (New Testament). The first time in **Romans 10:9,** as stated above, refers to salvation. The second time refers to the gifts of the Spirit.

I Corinthians 12:3

No one can say Yeshua is Lord without the inspiration of the Holy Spirit.

This confession is followed by the description of the nine charismatic gifts. If we are not submitted to Yeshua's lordship and authority, it would be unwise, even disastrous, to operate in prophetic gifts. When Nadav and Abihu, the sons of Aaron, offered strange fire on the altar, the fire of God killed them in a moment **(Leviticus 10:1-2).**

It is possible to try to operate in the charismatic gifts without submitting to Yeshua's authority. However, this situation is a grotesque contradiction in values. If a person wants to act by the "Holy" Spirit then his actions must be holy as well or at least holding to the most basic universal moral standards.

No one can really minister by the Holy Spirit and live in sin at the same time. This type of situation can only take place for a short time during which the person is being warned to repent before punishment comes. There is a period of overlap between the warning of conscience against the sin and the removal of the anointing. God always judges sin, but He normally allows for a period of warning before the punishment.

A good example of that is Samson. His strength stayed with him for a while during his sin, but ultimately it could not be sustained (**Judges 16:4-21**). Perhaps those around him wondered how someone who continually sinned with lust could possibly be used by God to do miracles. God was not authorizing the sin and anointing to "co-exist," but rather demanding that the sin be stopped. When Samson did not repent after the reasonable warning time, he was judged severely and the anointing removed.

If the person never repents, the situation may lead to missing salvation altogether. Here is what Yeshua said about trying to use spiritual power without submission to His authority:

Matthew 7:22-23

Many will say to me in that day, "Lord, lord, have we not prophesied in your name, and done many wonders in your name?" And then I will declare to them, "I never knew you; depart from me, you who practice lawlessness."

Is it possible to prophesy, evangelize and heal the sick while at the same time committing adultery, stealing money and lying? Unfortunately, yes; but only temporarily. When well-known charismatic figures sin, it obviously causes great problems for the faith of those who trusted in them.

It happens far more often than is tolerable. Yet, of course, the great majority of ministers of every stream of faith are primarily ethical and moral people. The number of ministers who do fall is a small percentage of the overall, yet their cases are usually publicized in a very scandalous way.

However, it is true that some people operate in the "supernatural," while their lives are not in right order and even overtly sinful or fraudulent. That is a fearful position. In God's eyes, that is like practicing witchcraft while using the name of Yeshua. (See the example of Simon the Sorcerer – **Acts 8:9-24**.)

What does the declaration that Yeshua is Lord mean? It is a commitment to doing Yeshua's will. Is it possible just to mouth the words and not mean it? Yes. When we declare that Yeshua is Lord, it must be with the full intention to do what He wants.

Matthew 7:21

Not everyone who says to me, "Lord, lord," will enter the kingdom of heaven, but the one who does the will of my father in heaven.

Let us declare Yeshua as our Lord: "Heavenly Father, I admit that I have done wrong and acted selfishly. I believe that Yeshua died for me on the cross that I might receive forgiveness of sins, and that He rose from the dead to give me eternal life. I open my heart to receive Him as lord. I commit myself to follow Yeshua and obey Him all the days of my life. Please fill me with the power and presence of your Spirit in love, purity and wisdom."

There are three general declarations of the lordship of Yeshua in the New Covenant. The first declaration of Yeshua's lordship is to receive eternal life (**Romans 10:9**); the second is to receive prophetic gifts (**I Corinthians 12:3**). There is a third declaration of lordship which deals with receiving spiritual authority (**Philippians 2:11**). We will continue with this third aspect in the next chapter.

QUESTIONS FOR REFLECTION:

Why is it important to see the cross as a tree?

What is the difference between Yeshua as Savior and Yeshua as Lord?

What is given to us through declaring Yeshua as Lord?

CHAPTER 5
REGAINING SPIRITUAL AUTHORITY

Yeshua's death on the cross was a test of His own obedience to God. Because He obeyed totally, even unto death, He proved Himself totally trustworthy; and, therefore, worthy to receive all authority.

His death on the cross also serves as a model for our own obedience, following His example. It is like a highway with two parallel lanes, each going in the opposite direction from the other. One lane is God's test for Yeshua to obey; the other is Yeshua's pattern for us to obey.

He received authority because He obeyed. We are to have the same attitude and mindset that He had. If Yeshua received authority through obedience, so will we receive authority together with Him through our obedience as well.

Philippians 2:5-11

Let this mind be in you which was also in Messiah Yeshua, who… made himself of no reputation, taking the form of a bond-servant… He humbled himself and became obedient to death, even the death of the cross. Therefore God has highly exalted him and given him the name which is above every name, that at the name of Yeshua every knee should bow, of those in heaven, and of those on earth and of those under the earth, and that every tongue will confess that Messiah Yeshua is Lord, to the glory of God the Father.

Since Yeshua obeyed unto death, everyone will have to recognize His authority and call Him "Lord." If we call Him "Lord," and follow in His footsteps, we will receive authority together with Him. The confession of Yeshua as Lord is to submit to His authority; this submission is the key to eternal life (**Romans 10:9**), prophetic gifts (**I Corinthians 12:3**), and spiritual authority (**Philippians 2:11**).

It is our destiny to have spiritual authority in God's kingdom. The first thing God did after He created Adam was to give him dominion and authority to rule over planet earth (**Genesis 1:26**). We were created to rule together with God. However, through sin, Adam relinquished his authority to the devil.

Since then every human being continues to relinquish his authority to the devil through sin (**Romans 5:12**). By the time Yeshua was born, Satan's authority was well established on this planet.

Luke 4:5-6

The devil took Yeshua up on a high mountain and showed him all the kingdoms of this world in a moment of time. The devil said to him, "All this authority and

their glory I will give to you, for it has been delivered to me, and I give it to whomever I want. Therefore, if you will worship before me, all will be yours."

This authority had not been given to the devil by God, but yielded and delivered to him by mankind. Satan stole it and usurped it from us. If Yeshua had also yielded to the devil, the devil would have remained victorious. If we continue to yield to the devil, he will continue to rob us of our destiny and rightful inheritance.

When Yeshua healed the sick and cast out demons, the people around Him understood that what was more important even than the supernatural healing and deliverance was the fact that God was giving enormous spiritual authority to this Man, and through Him that authority would be available to others. A prime example is the reaction of the disciples to the healing of the paralytic:

Matthew 9:8

The multitudes marveled and glorified God who had given such authority to men.

Luke 5:24

So that you may know that the Son of Man has authority on earth to forgive sins...

If we submit to Yeshua and resist the devil (**James 4:7; I Peter 5:6-9**), we can drive out the devil and regain the authority that was originally intended for us. We are not stealing authority from the devil; he stole it from us. Yeshua won back for us what God intended for us in the beginning.

In Yeshua, we can regain the spiritual authority that is our pre-destined portion. It already belongs to us. The devil stole it.

Yeshua won it back. We are re-possessing what was originally ours and now is rightfully ours again through Yeshua.

Human beings need a divine revelation even to understand that Yeshua has received spiritual authority and passed it on to us.

Ephesians 1:17-18

That the God of our Lord Yeshua the Messiah, the father of Glory, give you the spirit of wisdom and revelation in the knowledge of him, the eyes of your understanding being enlightened; that you may know what is the hope of his calling, what are the riches of the glory of his inheritance in the saints.

The revelation of the power that God has given us in Yeshua comes in parallel to what Yeshua did for us. The revelation of this inheritance comes in three parts:

1. On the cross, He gave us <u>forgiveness</u> of sins.

2. By His resurrection, He gave us eternal <u>life</u>.

3. In His ascension, He gave us spiritual <u>authority</u>.

Ephesians 1:19-23

What is the exceeding greatness of his power toward us who believe, which... he worked in Messiah when he raised him from the dead and seated him at his right hand in the heavenly places, far above all principality and might and dominion...

And put all things under his feet and gave him to be head over all things to the church, which is his body...

Yeshua was raised to the highest place of spiritual authority in the universe. He will exercise that authority through a governing body. That body is His body (the kehilah – ecclesia – church). He will govern the world through us (I Corinthians 6:2-3). If we submit to Him, then we become part of the group of people through whom He will rule the world.

This kind of spiritual authority is an extension of the prophetic authority that was given to the ancient Israelite prophets. For example, Jeremiah was given spiritual authority over the nations and kingdoms of his generation. **"Behold I have set you this day over the nations and over the kingdoms, to root out and to pull down, to destroy and to throw down, to build and to plant" – Jeremiah 1:10.** The same spiritual power over kingdoms and nations can be seen in the lives of Isaiah, Ezekiel, Samuel, Elijah, Elisha, Daniel, and others.

Submission is the key. Why? Because authority flows in **two directions:** *up and down.* Authority is submitted to upward and delegated to downward. To the degree that we submit to authority, to the same degree authority can be delegated to us.

It is such a simple principle that authority flows in two directions, both upward and downward. Yet it seems to be hidden from most people. It is the working principle of faith. One of the first people to see this was a Roman centurion (an officer responsible for 100 soldiers).

Luke 7:8-9

I am a man placed under authority, having soldiers under me. I say to one, "Go," and he goes; and to another, "Come," and he comes; and to my servant, "Do this," and he does it. When Yeshua heard these words, he was astonished at him. He turned to the

crowd and said, "I have not found such great faith, not even in Israel."

Yeshua was amazed that so many did not understand such a simple principle; and equally amazed that this Roman soldier could express this profound secret in such a clear and obvious way. The question is whether we comprehend it today.

Authority flows equally in two directions, upward and downward. It is like a mathematic equation or a principle of physics. What goes up, comes down. Authority is submitted to upward and delegated downward. If we submit to authority, it can be delegated to us.

God desires to delegate authority. Yeshua's first act after appointing the 12 disciples was to give them authority (**Luke 9:1**). Then when He appointed another 70 disciples, He gave them authority as well (**Luke 10:1**). God is searching for those who will rule and reign with Him in righteousness (**Romans 5:17; Revelation 5:10; 20:4, 6**).

This life constitutes a test for us from God. It is a test of faith and faithfulness; a test of trust and trustworthiness; a moral test; a test of integrity, love and obedience. If we pass the tests of this world, we will receive rewards in the world to come (**Matthew 5:12; 5:46; 6:4; 6:6; 6:18; Galatians 6:7; Hebrews 11:6**). Abraham passed the tests of God and became the father of faith to all believers (**Genesis 22:1; Romans 4:16**). Messiah Yeshua passed the ultimate test.

One of the rewards of God is authority. Not everyone will receive the same reward in the world to come. (For a description of "Rewards in Heaven," see Supplement 3.)

In the parable of the talents, Yeshua explained the principle that if we pass the tests in this world, we will receive greater delegated authority. A king gives different talents, abilities and authorities to his servants. He goes away to establish his kingdom authority. When he returns, he rewards those who have been faithful with different levels of authority.

Luke 19:17

Well done, good servant, because you were faithful in a very little, have authority over 10 cities.

Luke 19:19

Likewise you also will be over 5 cities.

The amount of authority you will have in the next world is determined by how you serve and submit in this world. Let us follow Yeshua's example and pass the tests of obedience that God places before us. Let us submit to Yeshua's authority and regain the authority that God originally planned for us (More on this topic in Chapter 24).

QUESTIONS FOR REFLECTION:

Explain the relationship between authority and submission.

What does it mean that "authority flows in two directions"?

How can you receive more God-given authority in this life?

CHAPTER 6
DOING GOD'S WILL

We are endeavoring to recover the original purpose and nature of authority. Because of sin and rebellion, our perception of authority has been perverted. We react to authority as something bad when it is supposed to be something good. Authority is good. Just to grasp this thought requires a renewal of the mind (**Ephesians 4:23**).

All authority comes from God. God is good. Therefore authority is good from its origin. However, world society is influenced by sin and rebellion (**I John 5:19**). Therefore God's authority is perverted on the one hand and rejected on the other. We must adjust our thinking to understand that God's will for us is good, desirable and perfect. We should run toward God's authority not away from it. God's authority is intended to bring into this world His blessing and good will for us.

Romans 12:2

Do not be conformed to this world, but be transformed by the renewing of your mind, so that you may prove what is the good, desirable and perfect will of God.

People tend to react negatively when they have to submit to authority. This can be demonstrated just by asking someone in a group or class to stand up and move to a different place. Even such a tiny request can cause irritation. Generally speaking, human beings do not like someone else telling them what to do.

God has a dilemma in dealing with the human race. He loves us and wants us to love Him in return. In order to give us the ability to love in return, He had to give us free will. Free will is a power that is individual and independent from anyone else. We enjoy this power and become irritable when we sense our freedom being impinged upon by the demands of others.

However, authority demands just the opposite: to do what someone else wants. I have to submit my will to someone else's will. The person with the authority is the one whose will is done.

Luke 6:46

Why do you call me, "Lord, lord," and not do the things which I say?

To call Yeshua Lord is to recognize His authority. Authority means that I will do what someone else says. To call Yeshua "Lord" and not do what He says is a contradiction in terms. We must train and discipline our wills to do God's will.

Our own will-power is like a wild animal, like a run-away horse that is out of control. We have to reign in that galloping horse and tame him. Part of the process of reigning in our wills can be done in prayer.

I try to pray every day what I call the 6-16-26 prayer; this is a series of three prayers taken from the gospel of Matthew, chapters 6, 16 and 26. Here is the first:

Matthew 6:10

Your kingdom come; your will be done on earth as it is in heaven.

This may be the most often repeated phrase of prayer in history. It seems so simple. Yet it is quite challenging and lies at the root of our discussion here about authority. We are asking God for His kingdom to come; for His will to be done. We are praying to resolve the conflict between God's will and mankind's disobedience.

His authority starts in heaven. It is good and perfect. It is coming down from heaven toward us on earth. The Lord's prayer is our offering ourselves to submit to God's kingdom authority. It is an invitation for His kingdom government to rule over the whole earth, as well as each individual.

James 1:17-18

Every good gift and every perfect gift is from above, and comes down from the Father of lights, with whom there is no variation or shadow of turning. By his own will he brought us forth...

James 3:17

The wisdom that is from above is first pure, then peaceable, gentle, willing to yield, full of mercy and good fruits, without partiality and without hypocrisy.

We are inviting His good and perfect will from above to come down into this world of human society. May His will, goodness and kingdom be done in our lives!

The decision to do His will takes place one person at a time. If I pray for God's will to be done on earth, it must first start with me. I need to pray for divine wisdom even to know what His will is (**Ephesians 1:17; James 1:5**). (See Supplement 4 – "Wisdom and the Fear of God.")

After I know what God's will is, I must wrestle my own will into submission to His. Here is the second prayer in the series:

Matthew 16:24

Whoever desires to come after me, let him deny himself, take up his cross [daily] and follow Me.

This prayer starts with a desire. We must first desire to follow after Yeshua, to be with Him, to act like Him, to obey Him, to become like Him.

Secondly, we must deny ourselves. Most of us would rather indulge ourselves than deny ourselves. We have our little selfish tendencies of pride, lust and laziness. However, real faith requires starting each day with self-discipline and self-denial.

This kind of self-denial is not self-destructive. A person who wants to win a gold medal must go through rigorous training and self-denial in order to reach the goal. The "self" we are denying here is our "selfishness." (The Bible also refers to this as "crucifying the flesh" – **Galatians 5:24**.)

This is self-denial for the sake of following after Yeshua, doing God's will and helping others. Self-denial in and of itself is merely religious exercise with no purpose. Denying self for the sake of winning God's higher goals is a quality of championship faith.

It means saying, "No" to our own fleshly desires. No one enjoys doing it, but there is no other way (II Timothy 2:3-7).

Here is the third of the 6-16-26 series: the astonishing prayer of Gethsemane. (See Supplement 5 – "Oil and Press.")

Matthew 26:39

O my Father, if it is possible, let this cup pass from me; nevertheless, not as I will, but as you will.

Yeshua is facing the most difficult decision in history. He will be turned over to evil religious and government leaders and experience betrayal, torture, humiliation, death, and the fires of hell. His motivation for all this was to obey His Father in heaven and to save human beings from death and hell.

This may be the single greatest moment of self-denial in all human history. Yeshua hated it; He fought within Himself: "Not My will, but Your will be done." This is the core of the decision which released all the power of God to save humanity.

Yeshua felt horrible at this moment; He shed blood, sweat and tears. He felt tired, alone, distressed, depressed, frustrated, dark, sad – in fact He had to struggle with about every negative feeling a human soul could experience. His closest disciples fell asleep and left Him to face this challenge alone (**Matthew 26:37-45, Luke 22:44**).

Yeshua asked His disciples at that time, and I believe He is still asking us now, "Is there anyone anywhere who will pray this kind of prayer with Me?" I imagine that it is difficult for God to find such people. There is a popular expression that "when the going gets tough, the tough get going." "Not my will be done but Yours" is a tough prayer for tough situations. Let's be among those who will pray as Yeshua did.

Spiritual laws and physical laws, generally speaking, operate by consistent patterns. The primary factor in the universe that changes from moment to moment is the human will. God will always be good and holy. The devil will always be evil. The flesh will always be selfish. Faith can move mountains and our words will come to pass (**Mark 11:23**). Whatever we sow, we will reap (**Galatians 6:7**). Gravity causes heavy objects to fall. Every action has a reaction; every cause has an effect.

The only variable is when a human being changes his will. Each person has 100% control over his own will and 0% control over someone else's. We change the world by changing our own will. God has enough power to force people to do what He wants, but He chooses not to do so. He calls us to submit voluntarily. His kingdom is not an evil dictatorship but a benevolent monarchy.

God will direct us like a conductor of a symphony orchestra. The player of each instrument in the orchestra must concentrate 100% to play the music exactly as written and exactly as led by the conductor. One slight mistake will ruin the beauty and harmony. But with years of rigorous practice and discipline, all the members of the orchestra, under the direction of the conductor, will produce extraordinary music.

Those who are in God's kingdom must live by voluntary submission to His authority. Those who must be forced into His kingdom will ultimately not take part. They will be forced "out." No one will be forced "in." Those in paradise will all be there voluntarily. Those in punishment will all have been forced to be there as a result of their refusing to submit their will to God's.

Let us align ourselves with God's benevolent and loving authority coming down from heaven. Now is the time to make a quality decision to go all the way to do God's will on earth even as Yeshua did.

QUESTIONS FOR REFLECTION:

How do we participate in God's will being done on earth?

Explain a biblical, non-destructive type of "denying yourself."

How does faith in God involve obedience to the laws of His kingdom?

CHAPTER 7
USING AUTHORITY TO BLESS

The purpose of authority is to bless. The very first thing God did after creating all the fish, birds and beasts was to bless them.

Genesis 1:22

And God blessed them, saying, "Be fruitful and multiply..."

Meditate on that for a moment. God creates all creatures with His power and then uses His authority to bless them. That is the original purpose of God's authority: to bless His creation.

The very first thing that God did when He created Adam and Eve was to bless them and give them authority at the same time. Creation, blessing, and the transfer of authority are integrally connected.

Genesis 1:26, 28

Then God said, "Let us make man in our image, according to our likeness. Let them have dominion over... all the earth." Then God blessed them, and said, "Be fruitful and multiply; fill the earth and subdue it; have dominion over the fish of the sea, over the birds of the air and over every living thing."

May we understand how profound the purposes of God were in this moment of creation! God's creating us contains His purpose for us, our first origins, and therefore our ultimate destiny. Why did God create you? Why do you exist? The biblical origin of man contains:

1. Being like God

2. Living on the earth

3. Being fruitful and multiplying

4. Having authority over creation

5. Blessing all of creation.

The purpose of authority is to bless. God used His power to create us. He used His authority to bless us. He created us in His image and gave us the authority to bless like He blessed. The combination of authority and blessing are at the heart of the original creation mandate.

Whether people know it or not, their innermost identity and desire is to be a human made in the likeness of God (like Yeshua), to exercise authority, to bless others, to take possession of the earth and live in it. It is in our biological and spiritual "DNA" as both men and women. (See Supplement 6 – "Creation and Dominion" by Youval Yanay.)

God blessed all of the animal creatures in **Genesis 1:22**. However, the animals were not made in God's image, so they could not bless others. Then God made us in His image, so we could extend His blessing to the creation and the creatures in it. God made us in His image in order to give us authority. He gave us authority in order to bless. We were created in His image to have authority in order to bless His creation. We were created to continue, extend and multiply God's blessing to all of creation. He gave us authority to fulfill that purpose.

God loves us and loves His creation and all of His creatures. He desires to bless and multiply His blessings. Authority is simply the ability to bless. Authority is a tool to bless. God gave us authority in order to use it as a blessing. He blessed us in order to bless others.

[**Note:** Similarly, God wants to prosper us so that we can prosper and bless others. The heart of generosity is more important than prosperity itself. See Supplement 7 – "The Generosity Gospel."]

The word for authority in Hebrew comes from the root *samach* - סמך, meaning to *lay hands on someone*. The very concept of authority is to lay one's hands on someone to bless them. (In addition, one must have hands laid on him by someone else to receive the impartation of authority in the first place.)

The ancient Israelite patriarchs understood their role as fathers in the image of God to bless their children. They would lay their hands on them and speak words of authority and blessing over them. Those words of authority and blessing with the laying on of hands would have eternal impacts.

In Jewish tradition, the fathers lay hands on the sons during the Aaronic blessing covering them with the prayer shawl (**tallit**) as a symbol of authority. That is a beautiful picture of fatherhood, authority, blessing and the laying on of hands.

God's first act at creation was to transfer authority. He is still looking to give away His authority today. He is looking for people to use His authority for the right purpose. The purpose of authority is to bless, protect, provide, nurture and edify. As soon as He can find people who desire that, He will give them authority.

God will only delegate authority to those who submit to authority. God is all-powerful. He doesn't need us to submit to Him. He is not in need of our help. He is all-loving and unselfish. He doesn't desire us to submit to Him for His own good. He desires us to submit to Him for our good. He desires to bless. He is not looking to hoard authority for Himself but to give authority away.

If we desire to bless others, then we will submit to God so that He can give us authority to bless. Paul (Saul) the apostle understood this principle. He spoke of his own authority this way:

II Corinthians 10:8

... the authority which the lord gave us for building you up, not for your destruction.

II Corinthians 13:10

... the authority which the lord has given me for building up and not for destruction.

Most people desire authority for their own good. That selfish desire for authority dominates the political arena, the business world, and, unfortunately, often times in our congregations of faith. However, it is possible to desire authority for pure reasons in order to bless others. That is the first requirement for leadership in the body of Messiah.

When we desire to use authority to bless others that position of authority becomes a good thing.

I Timothy 3:1

If a man desires the position of an overseer, he desires an excellent work.

Let us develop the kind of desire to bless people, to bless everyone, especially those in our families and in our local congregations. Those of us in positions of authority should use these positions to bless others. We who are husbands and fathers should use our authority to bless and protect our wives and children. Those who are employers should use their position to prosper and provide.

Authority for authority's sake does not interest us. Any glory or attention that may come to us is totally irrelevant and should be ignored. (This is why Yeshua warned us 3 times in the Sermon on the Mount not to do good works in order **"to be seen by men"** – **Matthew 6:1, 5, 16.**) But we do desire the tools to extend God's blessings to others. We desire for the body of Messiah, the *ecclesia*, to "be fruitful, multiply and fill the earth."

Words are the vehicles of expressing authority. God gave the ability to speak only to human beings. None of the animals can bless anyone else, only human beings can. Since we have the authority to bless, we also unfortunately have the ability to curse. Blessings and curses are conveyed primarily through words.

James 3:10

Out of the same mouth come forth blessing and cursing. My brothers, this should not be so.

Every person, no matter what their social position may be, has a measure of authority simply by the fact that they can speak words. Authority is expressed through words (whether in verbal decree or written statement). Until the person in authority speaks or writes the words, the authority is not put into effect. We speak words in God's image with a measure of God's authority. Let us use our ability for language to bless and edify those who hear us and not to curse or tear down (**Ephesians 4:29**).

This is so simple yet so profound: The purpose of authority is to bless; we use authority to build up. The reason for these two is that all authority comes from God and God is love (**I John 4:8**). The greatest kind of love is being willing to give our lives for another (**John 15:13**). Therefore the greatest authority comes from the willingness to give yourself to those over whom you have authority.

In speaking of the motivation of the good shepherd, Yeshua spoke of the willingness of the shepherd to give his life for the flock. In that context He spoke of authority: **"I give My life for the sheep. For this reason the Father loves Me – because I give My life and take it up again. I have authority to give it and I have authority to take it back." – John 10:15-18.** True authority comes from sacrificial love.

We all have authority over one thing: our own lives. If we love others, we are willing to give of ourselves for them. To the degree that we love others and are willing to give of ourselves for them, then God gives us authority over them for their benefit. Authority comes from love.

We could summarize the kind of authority that comes from God this way:

1. *Love is the basis of true authority*

2. *The purpose of authority is to bless*

3. *We use authority to build up others.*

Receiving authority from God and blessing His creation is what we were made to do. Let us fulfill our destiny to be God's agents of blessing and authority in this earth even as Yeshua did.

QUESTIONS FOR REFLECTION:

What is the purpose of authority?

How does God delegate authority? How can we receive it?

What were men and women originally created to do?

What is the origin of authority? How do we use it?

CHAPTER 8
UNDERSTANDING DELEGATED AUTHORITY

All authority originates with God and descends from Him. Because God is good, all authority in its origin is good. Since God wanted to extend and multiply His blessings exponentially throughout the human race, He immediately began to delegate authority to others. As authority is delegated to mankind, many kinds of problems emerge because men are sinful, selfish and often abusive. This has twisted the original purpose of authority.

Ecclesiastes 7:29

God made man upright, but they have sought out many schemes.

God made mankind righteous and good, but we have used our intellect, will-power and resources contrary to how God intended. To repair the righteous purpose of authority, we must understand the difference between two kinds of authority:

1. **Divine:** Direct *Spiritual Authority* from Heaven,

2. **Human:** Indirect *Delegated Authority* on Earth.

The first is perfect; the second is imperfect at best and sometimes evil. We can see the difference when Yeshua entered Jerusalem. He represented direct heavenly authority. The priests of the Temple, who had only delegated human authority, felt threatened and jealous.

Matthew 21:23

When he came into the Temple, the chief priests and the elders of the people confronted him… saying, "By what authority are you doing these things? Who gave you this authority?"

The question was quite reasonable, as the priests had authority from the Law of Moses, including the responsibility to manage the Temple. It was difficult for them to receive this Galilean street preacher, ex-carpenter, as having divine authority over them. They wanted to focus the question on which human institution had ordained His authority. However, Yeshua redirected the question to the real issue, which was the difference between the two kinds of authority.

Matthew 21:24-25

I will ask you one thing, which if you tell me, I will likewise tell you by what authority I do these things: The baptism of John – where was it from? - From heaven or from men?

There is tension here between prophetic and priestly authority. Yeshua challenged them that they in fact were resisting God's heavenly authority by acting only through their priestly institutional authority, while not recognizing divine, spiritual and prophetic authority. In this way, Yeshua indicated here that there are two sources of authority: one "from heaven" and one "from men."

[**Note:** This represented a continuation of the historic clash in ancient Israel between the priests and the prophets. The priests claimed institutional authority, while the prophets claimed inspirational authority. This tension existed from the times of the Mosaic Law and extended here into the Gospels as well.]

Within 24 hours, Yeshua is confronted again on a similar issue this time on the conflict with secular government authority. The Pharisees brought representatives of Herod's government to see if Yeshua would submit to this Gentile, ungodly authority.

Matthew 22:17

Is it lawful to pay taxes to Caesar, or not?

They are trying to trap Him. If He says, "Yes," they will accuse Him of submitting to paganism. If He says, "No," they will have Him arrested for treason against Rome. Yeshua rebukes them for their hypocrisy, but then turns to deal with the underlying issue. Must there be an inherent contradiction between direct spiritual authority from heaven and unrighteous authority of human government?

Although there would seem to be an obvious and irreconcilable conflict, Yeshua sees a place within which both types of authority can function. He reconciles the two. There is a place and a purpose for human government within its sphere of responsibility; and there is a place for divine spiritual authority over them.

Matthew 22:21

Render unto Caesar the things which are Caesar's, and unto God the things which are God's.

In one simple sentence that any child can understand, Yeshua succinctly resolves the profoundly complex issue of the seemingly unresolvable conflict between spheres of divine and delegated authority. The conflict between the two kinds of authority seems irreconcilable to us, but to God it is possible.

The conflict arises yet a third time, just a day or so later. After the Passover Seder and Yeshua's arrest, He is brought before Pilate, the cruel and powerful governor from Rome. Pilate is stunned that Yeshua makes no effort to defend Himself. Pilate interprets Yeshua's silence as belittling his authority.

John 19:10

Are you not speaking to me? Do you not know that I have authority to crucify you, and the authority to release you?

Of course, Yeshua did know. But He knew that He was obeying spiritual authority from heaven, which was superior to the earthly government of Pilate, no matter how powerful it seemed. What may seem even more surprising is that Yeshua recognized Rome's government as a legitimate delegated authority established by God, despite the injustices involved.

John 19:11

You could have no power at all against me unless it had been given you from above.

Yeshua recognized Pilate's position of authority. Pilate is on the verge of making an unjust decision. However, Yeshua is not worried. Ultimately, there is divine authority over and above Pilate's government. If Pilate does wrong, he will have to give account to that divine authority on Judgment Day and face his own punishment.

Yeshua sees the injustice about to be done as a temporary and limited problem. Sooner or later all injustices will be corrected by divine authority above. Pilate is the one having a problem, not Yeshua! That pagan governor felt the moral clarity of Yeshua's words, and while he did not want to admit it, he knew Yeshua was right. From that moment on, Pilate sought a way to avoid having to judge Yeshua.

Ecclesiastes 5:8

If you see the oppression of the poor, and the violent perversion of justice and righteousness in a province, do not marvel at the matter; for high official watches over high official, and higher officials are over them.

King Solomon recognized the same pattern. There are multiple levels of human authority. Human government has much injustice, violence and corruption. However, ultimately all human authority must give a moral account to the divine authority which allowed them to have their position in the first place.

We need to fight for moral and social justice because it is right to do so. The prophets of Israel harshly criticized the kings and government leaders for injustice. Their concern was not for their own personal well-being. They trusted in a higher power of eternal, divine justice. We fight for social justice for the sake of those who are suffering now.

While we fight for issues of social justice, we do not fight against the government institution itself. We fight to correct the injustice not to overthrow the government. It is a difficult moral balance to oppose social injustice without rebelling against the government itself. We need to discern the spiritual issues beyond the political conflicts, whether left wing or right wing.

In the Israeli Knesset there is always an opposition coalition fighting fiercely against the Prime Minister. Political leaders certainly have the right to bring criticism when issues of social justice are violated. However, for the opposition to set itself to cause the government's downfall does not seem like a godly or biblical stance to me.

Only Yeshua can fully repair the dichotomy between heavenly and earthly authority because only He has authority in both realms.

Matthew 28:18

All authority has been given to me in heaven and earth.

The reconciliation between these two realms of authority touches on the original purpose of creation and the relationship between God and man. Ultimately, Yeshua will bring them both together into one.

Ephesians 1:10

In the fullness of time, God will bring together in one all things in Messiah, both which are in heaven and which are on the earth.

May God grant us the wisdom to discern the differences between heavenly and earthly authority, and to understand His plan for the ultimate reconciliation and unification between the two!

QUESTIONS FOR REFLECTION:

Where does all authority come from?

What are the inherent conflicts in relating to delegated spiritual authority?

When it comes to the injustices of human government, what can bring comfort to us as followers of Yeshua?

PART TWO:
SPHERES OF AUTHORITY

CHAPTER 9
DEFINING SPHERES OF AUTHORITY

Whenever authority is delegated, it must be clearly defined as to its extent and sphere. No delegated authority is unlimited. Authority is only to be in effect within its defined sphere. When authority tries to reach beyond its sphere, that authority becomes illegitimate.

II Corinthians 10:13-14

We will not boast beyond measure, but within the limits of the sphere in which God has appointed us – a sphere which especially includes you. We are not over-extending ourselves, as though our authority did not extend to you.

Notice Paul's use of the words: *measure, limit, sphere, appointed, include, extend, over-extend.* He recognized that his authority was limited to the congregations within his sphere. He did not try to extend his authority to others not within that sphere. The definition of who was in his area of responsibility was quite clear to him.

Human authority has limits and borders. Each authority has its own sphere. Each sphere of authority has its own rules of operation.

Delegated human authority on earth falls into four basic spheres or categories:

1. Family

2. Employment

3. Government

4. Church/Synagogue

[**Note:** These categories are a bit over-simplified and can be even more complex when dealing with Islamic, Catholic, Jewish, and Communist societies. Nevertheless, the four categories are a helpful model to simplify and clarify our understanding about realms of authority.]

In each of these four categories, authority flows in the two directions – upward and downward – as mentioned earlier in the example of the centurion (**Luke 7:8-9**). We submit to authority upward and delegate authority downward. There are multiple levels of authority within each sphere with God's divine authority over all.

All four categories are limited to the borders of their spheres horizontally; if they try to extend themselves across those boundaries into the others' spheres, there is immediate conflict.

Therefore, all human authority must be limited, for God is always over and above all authority. Human authority is secondary. He is the "captain" – meaning "the head." We are in position as a "lieutenant" – meaning "taking his place." We are not God; we only represent Him.

Whenever we are under someone else's authority, we should respect his position because God has allowed him to be there for the time being. Whenever we are in a position of authority, we should maintain humility and the fear of God, because we will ultimately have to give God an account for our use of that authority.

Human authority is limited because it has a defined area, a realm with boundaries. No one has "all" authority except Yeshua. Each nation, church/congregation, business and family has its own borders.

Human authority is limited because we respect the free will and conscience of every other human being, even as God does.

Human authority is limited because all of us have sinned. Since our righteousness is impaired, our power must be limited as well.

Finally, human authority is limited because each person can have access to God in his own heart through the Holy Spirit.

Let us summarize. Human authority is limited, because:

1. God is over us vertically

2. Spheres have boundaries horizontally

3. Everyone has free will

4. Everyone has sinned

5. Everyone has access to God.

However, given these limitations, God does exercise delegated authority over human affairs to humans through the four categories of family, workplace, government, and church. Let's look at some examples.

[**Note:** The principles of relationships and authority in these categories are described more fully in the book "*Covenant Relationships*," chapters 24 to 32. The purpose here is only to give a brief outline to define those spheres of authority.]

I. Family

Parents have authority over the children; the husband has authority over the wife. Yeshua has authority over the husband. When a child is married, a new sphere of authority is reestablished in his or her new family. The parents become grandparents. Their role decreases to that of an advisor, while the young parents take the primary authority with their own children.

When the Bible speaks of a man having authority over a woman, it is within the marriage context. I do not have authority over anyone else's wife or any other woman. A man has authority only with his own wife or with his daughters until they are married.

If asked whether my wife must submit to me, I would answer, "Yes, then yes and no, then no." As my wife's husband, 1 am her full authority within the family structure. So, "yes" I do have authority over her. (Although as some husbands have humorously commented, "I always have the last word in our home – 'Yes, dear.'")

I would not recommend a man to marry a woman if she was not willing to recognize his spiritual authority as husband; nor vice versa. As it is written:

Ephesians 5:22

Wives, submit to your husbands, as to the Lord.

The principle of submission of wife to husband is repeated in **I Corinthians 11:3, I Corinthians 14:35, Colossians 3:18, I Timothy 2:11-12** and **I Peter 3:1-6**. Notice that the wife submits with the condition that it is "as unto the Lord." Yeshua has authority over both the husband and the wife. The husband does not have absolute authority but limited, delegated authority.

Notice as well the verse immediately preceding:

Ephesians 5:21

… submitting to one another in the fear of God.

In this verse husband and wife are to submit to one another. Therefore: "yes and no." Sometimes I submit to my wife; sometimes she submits to me. Husbands and wives are equal, mutually submissive brothers and sisters before God their father.

My wife is totally submitted to me in my role as her husband. She is sort of a male chauvinist's dream-come-true. Before our wedding, she memorized and recited to me **Proverbs chapter 31** about the virtuous woman and committed herself to live by its standards. She has certainly done that.

However, she is submitted first to God. Her commitment is to Yeshua before it is to me. In that sense, "no," my wife is not ultimately submitted to me at all but only to the Lord. She is serving Him through her devotion and submission to me. She is submitted to me only as I am "unto the Lord."

This creates a harmonious three-way balance of authority and submission.

1. Each person is submitted first to the Lord

2. Each person is submitted mutually one to another

3. Each person is submitted to the delegated authority in its sphere.

This balance of authority can be seen in other spheres as well.

II.   Employment

Authority within the workplace is perhaps the easiest to define since it normally is contained within specified work hours, at a work location, according to a defined job description and with a clear hierarchy of management. In the workplace, we often find ourselves in positions of authority as management and at the same time under higher managers. Here it is easy to see the principles of authority working in both directions.

The boss or employer should certainly not see himself as taking the position of authority given to the family or the church. However, in communist societies, the work place was often joined with the government to usurp the authority of the nuclear family and the religious congregation.

We as believers in Yeshua should be the best employees because we recognize that the position of employer is a delegated authority from God.

[**Note:** Of course in ancient times there were slaves and masters. We are drawing a parallel to modern employers and employees. The contractual basis of employment in modern democratic societies most likely represents a godly step forward in limiting the sphere of employer authority as opposed to the almost total dominion a master had over a slave in Roman society 2,000 years ago.]

Ephesians 6:5

Servants, be obedient to those who are your masters according to the flesh

(This commandment is repeated in **Colossians 3:22**.) A boss at work cannot tell a wife how to treat her husband, nor a citizen how to vote, nor a believer how to pray. The employer has authority within the activities of the employment contract.

The same biblical passages telling the employee to submit to the employer also warn the employer not to abuse his authority. As followers of Yeshua, we should be the best kind of employers because we respect each of the employees as a child of God, and we know that we must give account to God for our actions. Each person has a role to play as an agent or steward of God's resources.

Ephesians 6:9

You, masters, do the same things to them, giving up threatening, knowing that your own Master also is in heaven.

Colossians 4:1

Masters, give your bondservants what is just and fair, knowing that you also have a Master in heaven.

Once again we find this same healthy and harmonious balance of authority. God is over all. Authority is delegated within defined spheres. Those under authority should submit. Those in authority should have humility and the fear of God knowing they are serving in a delegated, temporary position and will soon have to give moral account to the Greater Authority.

QUESTIONS FOR REFLECTION:

What are the four spheres of earthly authority?

Who has the only unlimited authority?

What are the limits of a wife's submission to the husband?

Why is the employment sphere in a free society easy to define?

CHAPTER 10
LIMITING GOVERNMENT POWER

We are continuing our definition of the four spheres of delegated human authority: Family, Employment, Government, Church/ Congregation.

III.   Government

Each government is confined to a sphere of jurisdiction, whether that be a city, state or country. A government leader has no authority in a different jurisdiction. The prime minister of Italy has no authority in Spain. The mayor of London has no authority in Paris. The European Union has no authority in the United States.

[**Note:** In the light of biblical prophecy, we should most likely be in favor of limiting authority in the United Nations. God has not given authority to any organization to rule over all the nations. An overarching international federation of governments would be dangerous. The sovereignty of individual nations should be protected.]

Governments have authority in issues dealing with political and civil affairs. They do not have authority within the family. That's why we are in favor of laws that protect family values and prevent government interference within the nuclear family on family issues.

Family authority is also limited: while parents have the right to spank their children in moderation, beating a child in brutality would cross the boundary line and become a type of criminal activity. There is a clear moral distinction between right and wrong application of parental authority.

Neither do governments have authority within the church. That's why we are in favor of the separation of church and state. Separation of church and state does not mean keeping biblical faith out of secular institutions. Rather it is to protect churches and congregations from government control.

Separation of church and state was designed to guarantee freedom of religious expression, not to limit it. The principle of separation of church and state has sometimes been twisted to the point of having the secular government promote atheism in schools and prevent freedom of religious expression in the public realm.

The second purpose of separation of church and state was to keep powerful religious institutions from controlling the civil government or silencing other independent expressions of faith. That happened in the Holy Roman Empire overseen by the Catholic Church in the Middle Ages. It happens today in almost all countries where a radical Islamic group has gained power, which immediately outlaws all other types of religious expression.

Separation of religion and state authority has also been problematic in Israel with the leverage of orthodox Jewish parties in the government coalitions, and their monopoly of Jewish religious rituals and institutions within the country.

Our understanding of the biblical worldview leans towards limiting the power of an overly centralized civil government. Government cannot solve fundamental world problems because the roots of human problems are not political but spiritual and moral. Power must be limited with checks and balances because men are sinful and tempted to corruption by power without restraints.

As the Reformation spread across Europe and the gospel into America, biblical principles were sought to reform government structure as well. The idea of "covenant" in the Bible led to the development of government charters, such as the American Constitution. Constitutionally-based, democratic republics became a positive framework for many Western governments.

How do we apply the biblical worldview of the balance between divine and delegated authority to the structure of civil government? Here are a few principles:

1. **Religious Freedom** – Since God's spiritual authority is above political government, the first issue is to guarantee freedom of religious expression. (See Supplement 8 – "Religious Liberty" by Dan Juster.)

2. **Constitutional Base** – Definitions of power for the government should be written down so that the power can be limited and not cross those defined boundaries. Government power must be limited by the "rule of law" to its appointed sphere. That sphere must be well defined. This is the purpose of a constitution, written laws and a politically independent judiciary.

3. **Family Values** – Since the family is a separate sphere of authority from the civil government, the

government should be restricted from interfering with parental authority and respect traditional moral, marital and family values within the realm of parental authority.

4. **Free Enterprise** – Since the employment sphere is also different from the government sphere, the principle of free enterprise should be upheld. This is not a political/economic issue of socialism versus capitalism, but a division of authority to prevent government from overextending its power. Government and business are two separate spheres. We do not want business to control the government, nor the government to control business. Just as there is separation between church and state, so should there be separation between state and business. Business influence over the government brings corruption. Money is a form of power. Government is a form of power. For the safety of all, these two should be restricted from both directions.

5. **Democratic Republic** – Democracy respects the free will of the individual; the republic respects the principle of delegated authority. Democracy by itself is imbalanced. (More discussion of this below.)

6. **Checks and Balances** – Government should be divided into three realms: judicial, legislative and executive. The three functions hold one another in check, keeping the other from gaining too much authority. When there is a balance between the three, there is safety. These three spheres of government can be derived from **Isaiah 33:22 – "YHVH our judge, YHVH our lawmaker,**

YHVH our king; He is our savior." The judge is the judicial branch; the lawmaker is the legislative branch; the king is the executive branch. God is all of those and above all. When divine authority is delegated to men, it is best to divide the three functions.

[**Note:** In Isaiah 33:22, the one who has authority in all three realms is YHVH. God is the ultimate judge, lawmaker and king. This YHVH God is also prophesied in this passage as "our savior." Ultimately, in reverse, this divine savior will become the leader of our government in all three spheres. Messiah gave us the Law; will be Judge on the day of resurrection; and King over the earth in the millennial kingdom. Until then, we need clear checks and balances in our civil government.]

7. **Moral Absolutes** – Regardless of one's religious or political background, basic moral absolutes must be taught in every realm of society. The Ten Commandments set those standards. Yeshua emphasized 5 of them as the minimum moral absolutes: **"Do not murder; do not commit adultery; do not steal; do not bear false witness; honor your father and mother"** **– Matthew 19:18-19.** This principle precedes Jewish or Christian religious beliefs and defines universal moral values of the human conscience. If these are not clearly taught, then any form of government will tends toward corruption.

[**Note:** The founders of the American government did a good job in establishing a tripartite, constitutional democratic republic. However, I think too much was invested in the office of the Presidency. The King in ancient societies had too much power. A positive reformation of this position is to split the King's authority into two roles. In many countries around the world, the primary governing authority is given to the Prime Minister, where there remains a more figurative role above him as a King or President. Having the head of the government split into two positions of a figurative King or President above the position of the Prime Minister as the central governing authority, seems to be a proper application of biblical principles to my view.]

Are we in favor of democracy? Yes, but only in a democratic republic based on a constitution defining and limiting government powers, and guaranteeing judicial procedure, traditional family values and religious freedom. Democratic elections alone will not bring a solution. Democracy is simply the vote of the people. The vote of the people is an important element in the triangle of balance of power.

However public opinion also tends toward corruption. The right, most moral decision is often in the minority. (**"Do not go after a crowd to do wrong; and do not respond to the majority to turn aside, or after many people to twist justice"** – Exodus 23:2.) The minority opinion is often the morally and judicially correct decision.

The Nazi party was voted in democratically in Germany in 1933, and then went on the road to the destruction of Europe and genocide of the Jews. Communist governments have been voted in, which then went on to rob all basic religious and economic freedom. Western countries today have democratic elections, but are losing their Judeo-Christian moral foundations, and thus are sinking into financial corruption, family disintegration and sexual decadence.

This has been a problem with the West's approach to Islam. The West has pushed democratic elections as a solution to the Islamic world, yet without the demand for religious freedom and judicial process. Moderate Islam is usually followed by radical Islam. When a radical Islamic government is voted into power, almost all freedoms are outlawed, and a Sharia dictatorship takes over. Islamic democracy has been satirically called, "One man, one vote, one time."

In some of the Islamic countries (such as Egypt and Turkey), the army tended to safeguard economic stability and religious freedom in opposition to radical Islamic takeover. The lack of Western understanding of radical Islam and the role of the military allowed some of these nations to be taken over by an Islamic dictatorship through a "democratic" election that then immediately destroyed all democratic values, freedoms and judicial institutions.

End time prophecies describe the ultimate form of evil as the one-world religious government of the anti-Christ (**Revelation 13**). We who believe in biblical values recognize God's delegated authority in government; yet, it should be limited to its proper sphere with the proper checks and balances, along with the guarantee of religious freedom, social justice and basic moral values.

The biblical world view of human sinfulness, religious freedom, moral conscience, independence of the nuclear family, judicial process and end-times' prophecies of an evil one-world government points to the need to limit centralized government power.

May God give us wisdom to respect those in government authority, yet recognize the limitations of government power! May He grant us the courage and discernment to demand moral integrity of those in office (and rebuke them publically when moral standards are broken)! And may He give wisdom to those in authority to rule in justice and righteousness!

QUESTIONS FOR REFLECTION:

What are the primary purposes of "the separation of church and state"?

What are the seven principles of civil government that help balance divine and delegated authority?

Why is democracy alone not enough to guarantee justice in government?

CHAPTER 11
PROTECTING THE FLOCK

In continuing our discussion of the four categories of delegated authority on earth, let us read again Paul's words that authority comes in defined spheres or areas of service and responsibility.

II Corinthians 10:13-14

We will not boast beyond measure, but within the limits of the sphere in which God has appointed us – a sphere which especially includes you. We are not over-extending ourselves, as though our authority did not extend to you.

As there are spheres and levels of authority in the family, business and government, so there are as well in the fourth category: the church or local congregation.

IV.   Congregation

When we use the word *church,* or *kehilah* in Hebrew, or *ecclesia* in Greek, we can refer to several dimensions. In the highest dimension, it is a group of people who are seated supernaturally spiritually in heaven above all power and principality.

Ephesians 1:19-23

What is the exceeding greatness of his power toward us who believe, which... he worked in Messiah when he raised him from the dead and seated him at his right hand in the heavenly places, far above all principality and might and dominion...

And put all things under his feet and gave him to be head over all things to the church, which is his body...

Ephesians 2:6

...raised us up together, and made us sit together in the heavenly places in Messiah Yeshua.

In this sense the *ecclesia* is a spiritual body of people, who are above the realm of human authority, serve as an intermediary between Yeshua's heavenly authority and the delegated authority on earth. Yeshua has all authority in heaven and on earth (**Matthew 28:18**). He sits in heaven at God's right hand - the position of highest authority in the universe. Earthly authority is delegated into the hands of people on earth. The *ecclesia* is the spiritual bridge between the two.

The *church-kehilah-ecclesia* is also the worldwide Body of Messiah; it is the total composite body of people, which includes everyone on earth who has received Yeshua as Lord.

In this section I want to address the third aspect of **church-kehilah-ecclesia**, which is the local congregation of believers in all the different locations around the world. We will call this a "congregation."

In the local congregation, there is delegated authority. There are a variety of ways to look at authority within the congregation, but let's try to simplify it into three basic levels: deaconate, eldership, five-fold ministry.

The deacons are responsible for areas of service in the congregation. The first deacons were appointed at the congregation in Jerusalem when it started to grow (**Acts 6:1-7**). Deacons are seen as an office of authority and are responsible for overseeing service in the congregation under the authority of the elders (**I Timothy 3:8-12**). The operative word involved is "serving." (For fuller description about deacons, see *Covenant Relationships*, chapter 32 – "Deaconate: the Gift of Service.")

The elders have primary responsibility for the management and oversight of the local congregation. In every description of a local congregation, the elders are seen as having authority (**Acts 6:6; 20:17; 15:4, 6, 22, 23; I Timothy 3:1-7; 4:14; Titus 1:5; I Peter 5:1, 5; Hebrews 13:7**). One of the purposes of eldership authority in the congregation is to protect the members from spiritual dangers, false teachers and destructive people.

Acts 20:28-29

Take heed to yourselves and to all the flock among which the Holy Spirit has made you overseers, to shepherd the congregation... For I know that after my departure, savage wolves will come in among you, not sparing the flock.

The job of the elders and shepherds is to protect the flock. (For fuller description about elders, see *Covenant Relationships*, chapter 29 – "Eldership: Congregational Government.")

It has become popular in some circles today to say that there is no need to meet in a congregation, but just in an informal group of believers. Small group meetings for food and fellowship is a central aspect of congregational life (**Acts 2:46**), but it does not replace the wider aspects of congregational life. What is the difference between a "group" and a "congregation?" The answer is: eldership.

A congregation is part of the greater Body of Messiah. The local congregation and the greater Body is a group of people with authority and under authority. First it is under the absolute authority of Yeshua; secondly it is under the delegated authority of elders. Those who want only an informal group often mean they want a group without elders. Or on the other hand they may feel that they have not been able to find elders who are trustworthy.

However, the *ecclesia* is essentially a group with authority: first under Yeshua's lordship, and secondarily under eldership authority. It is essential that those elders be trustworthy, submitted to God in their own lives, and fulfill the basic moral and relational requirements listed in **I Timothy 3:1-13.** This chapter defines the basic standards for eldership. These moral and relational requirements must come before the impartation of authority to any person.

Yeshua is building his *ecclesia-kehilah* in the earth. From the first mention of the building of the church, Yeshua imparted to it authority. A congregation without authority is not yet fully a New Covenant congregation.

Matthew 16:18-19

You are Peter, and on this rock I will build my church, and the gates of hell will not prevail against it. And I will give you the keys of the kingdom of heaven, and whatever you bind on earth will be bound in heaven, and whatever you loose on earth will be loosed in heaven.

Peter had a revelation that Yeshua is the Messiah. Immediately Yeshua called him to start building the *ecclesia* and at, the same time, delegated to him authority. The keys and the binding and loosing are symbols of authority. Then Yeshua also informed them that they would be attacked by the forces (gates) of hell. These elements could be summarized as:

1. Revelation of Yeshua

2. Building the Congregation

3. Spiritual Authority

4. Demonic Attack.

The elders have authority like shepherds and are supposed to protect the flock. One of the primary purposes of authority is to protect the weak. Authority serves to protect. Young believers need to be members in a congregation with elders in order not to be left unprotected and exposed to demonic attack.

Just as judges protect from corruption; police protect from criminals; soldiers protect from foreign enemies; parents protect their children from harm; so, are elders supposed to protect the members of the congregation from spiritual attack and build them up in faith and love as followers of Yeshua.

It would have been unheard of among the first-century disciples for someone not to join a local congregation and receive the spiritual authority within that congregation. The logic was simple: if you receive Yeshua as lord, you join the group of people He is lord over. If you submit to Yeshua's authority, you also submit to those to whom He has delegated authority.

Acts 2:47

The Lord added to the church daily those who were being saved.

Believing in Yeshua and joining the congregation were seen as one and the same. Joining the congregation included receiving the authority within the congregation.

The third level of authority in the *ecclesia* is comprised of the "five-fold gift" ministers. This is the senior group of leaders who function in the offices of apostle, prophet, evangelist, pastor and teacher.

Ephesians 4:11-12

He gave some to be apostles, some prophets, some evangelists, and some pastors and teachers, for the equipping of the saints for the work of ministry, for the edifying of the body of Messiah.

The deacons take responsibility for areas of service within the local congregation. The elders govern and protect the local congregation. The apostolic or "five-fold" ministry group provides leadership for the wider body. They are responsible for "building up the body of Messiah." These senior leaders must also take part in elders' level government within the local body.

There is a healthy dynamic tension between the local pastors and elders who are focusing on the needs of the local congregation and the "five-fold" leadership teams who are focusing on the wider body.

The question then arises to whom do these senior leaders submit? I have seen this work successfully several times in groups of a small number of senior leaders who meet together for fellowship, personal sharing and mutual accountability.

I was once acquainted with a group of five senior pastors in Korea who would meet twice a year. (Each one led a church of over 20,000 people.) I asked one of them what they talked about in their times together. He mentioned that a common topic was "How to finish well." In other words they all knew that despite their huge successes, no one is insusceptible to sin. They wanted to help one another not to "blow it" in the final stretch of the race.

In our group at Tikkun International, we meet about twice a year with our senior leaders (Dan Juster, Eitan Shishkoff, David Rudolph, Paul Wilbur and myself). For our team at Revive Israel, we meet once a month for teamwork strategy, trust building and accountability. We try to be as open with one another as possible, confess faults and receive prayer one for another. In this way, there is at least a sense of mutual submission and accountability.

(We will discuss these five ministry offices further in chapter 20.)

QUESTIONS FOR REFLECTION:

What are the three spheres or dimensions of the ecclesia?

What are the three levels of authority within the local congregation?

Why is it important for believers to meet in elder-led congregations?

CHAPTER 12
TAKING RESPONSIBILITY

All leadership starts with taking responsibility for an area of service within the local congregation. In Yeshua's kingdom all leadership is based on sacrificial love and serving in humility.

In the mid 1990's we were able to launch the Messianic Jewish Alliance of Israel as an officially registered, Israeli, non-profit organization in order to handle its finances and administration. Ilan Zamir, a dear brother who has gone on to be with the Lord, served as president; I worked on the administration as secretary of the board.

One of our early projects was to establish a closed email chat network in order to encourage unity and communication among the leaders. (Our friend Michael Enos engineered the network and continues to do the tech administration for it today.) The network turned out to be highly successful and became the primary communication tool among Israeli Messianic leaders today.

We ran into what seemed to be a small problem: who is allowed to be on the network? That little problem turned out not to be very easy to solve. Almost every person perceives himself as a leader. (See Supplement 9 – "Exception to the Rule.") We did not want to take on the responsibility or the authority to determine who is a leader in the Israeli Messianic body. All we wanted was a guideline as to who could sign up for the email list.

The problem wouldn't go away. In fact, the problem seemed to be getting bigger. The board discussed the issue repeatedly. Eventually, we split the list into two levels: one for elders and one for deaconate level.

The elder network (ZKN), we defined as: *one who is an ordained elder in an established local congregation.* The general network (GMN) we defined as: *one who is responsible for a significant area of service in a local congregation.* It was surprising to note that many people saw themselves as national leaders but were not ordained local elders. There were also many who were not taking responsibility for any area of service in a local congregation.

This touches on two central issues of leadership and authority: service and responsibility. Simply put: 1) *leadership arises out of service;* and 2) *authority is equal to responsibility.* One who does not serve is not a leader; one who has no area of responsibility has no real authority.

Matthew 20:25-27

The rulers of the Gentiles lord it over them, and those that are great exercise authority over them. Yet it shall not be so among you; whoever desires to become great among you let him be your servant. Whoever desires to be first among you, let him be your slave.

Yeshua's style of leadership is *servant leadership.* This is a reverse value of the world system where a leader wants to have others serve him. In Yeshua's kingdom, the more one serves, the more he is a leader. The issue is an attitude of heart. A leader must lead and delegate to others; but, he must continue with a servant attitude.

Taking responsibility is the next step. It is more than service; it is making sure that an area of service will be done. It is easier to find people to serve in a given task than it is to find people who will take responsibility for an area of service.

If a leader has served much, he knows how to do the work of service. He looks for other people to help in order to multiply the fruit. Therefore, he must delegate work. Normally the leader could do the task more effectively and efficiently than others. If he asks someone to do a task, then the task is done, but the responsibility returns to him.

One person doing one task does not relieve the leader from much of the weight of responsibility. When a person is willing to take responsibility for an area of service, even a small area of service, it is a huge benefit. Then the overall weight of responsibility is shared and the burden on the leadership is lessened.

First, we need people who are willing to serve. Then we need people who are willing to take responsibility for an area of service, no matter what the size. The measure of authority is equal to the measure of responsibility. One who takes responsibility for a wider area of service has a higher level of authority. There is no authority without responsibility. The level of authority is determined by the level of responsibility.

This is the challenge of leadership: finding people who are willing to take responsibility. Taking responsibility means there must be an area to be taken responsibility over. That area needs to be defined. The sphere of responsibility becomes the sphere of that person's authority. Let's look once more at how Paul defined his sphere of authority:

II Corinthians 10:13-14

We will not boast beyond measure, but within the limits of the sphere in which God has appointed us – a sphere which especially includes you. We are not over-extending ourselves, as though our authority did not extend to you.

The sphere of authority is equal to the area of responsibility. It should be noted that responsibility comes before authority and service before responsibility. The process of leadership is three steps:

1. Serving with humility

2. Taking an area of responsibility

3. Receiving sphere of authority.

We serve first and receive authority later. As we are serving and taking responsibility for an area of service, the granting of authority is assigned to match the sphere.

In Yeshua's kingdom, authority is not "taken;" it is given. It is given by someone who had the authority before. Authority is delegated from one who has authority and received by the one coming into the place of authority. Notice the word "given" in our theme verse:

Matthew 28:18

All authority has been given to me in heaven and on earth.

Yeshua earned that authority rightfully. It was given to Him by His Father in heaven. He did not "take" the authority but received what was given to Him. Then He turned around and gave it to those who were under His authority.

Matthew 28:19

Go, therefore, and make disciples of all the nations.

Yeshua is transferring authority to His disciples in His name. Actually He is more than delegating authority – He is leaving! He is transferring to them responsibility for His entire life mission. He is asking them to take responsibility for everything that will happen with His kingdom on earth. That is an astounding transfer of authority.

Yeshua had been planning to leave and transfer all responsibility to His disciples from the first moment He met them. They went through a training process from being disciples to being apostles. As disciples, they served Him. As apostles, they continued to serve even more by taking responsibility for carrying on His mission.

Luke 9:30-31

Moses and Elijah appeared in glory and spoke with him about his departure.

On the Mount of Transfiguration, in front of His disciples, Moses and Elijah spoke with Yeshua about His "departure." The word in Greek here is *exodus.* (Symbolically Yeshua's crucifixion, resurrection and ascension were seen as spiritual fulfillment of the exodus of the children of Israel from Egypt.)

Yeshua's ascension to heaven was a departure, an exodus, an **exit.** Yeshua had planned His "exit strategy" from the beginning. This is profound. Everything Yeshua did in teaching and discipleship was to equip His disciples to take His place. He did not build His ministry to rest only on Himself. From the first, He planned for them to share everything with Him.

Yeshua's example is helpful to build a strategy for growth and multiplication. A leader should purpose to build every area of ministry not to be dependent on himself or his personal talents alone. We seek from the first moment to find others to disciple and train so that they may take ownership of the vision and move it forward. We must plan our exit strategy from the beginning.

The kingdom multiplies as we train others and then pass the vision and authority onto them. The process of discipleship is to get them ready to receive the authority. We disciple others first to serve, then take responsibility, then receive authority, and then eventually make the vision their own and multiply it forward.

QUESTIONS FOR REFLECTION:

What is the starting point for all leadership?

What are the two central issues of leadership and authority?

What are the three steps of the leadership process?

What is the purpose of the process of discipleship?

CHAPTER 13
HONORING SPIRITUAL FATHERS

In chapter 2 we learned that the Ten Commandments teach that parents can pass both good and bad characteristics to their children. The bad we call curses; the good we call blessings. The fact that two of the Ten Commandments deal with the transfer of spiritual blessings shows just how important the issue is.

Deuteronomy 5:9

... visiting the sins of the parents upon the children.

Deuteronomy 5:16

Honor your father and your mother that your days might be long and that it might be well with you upon the land.

In chapter 2 we also dealt with breaking the curses and being healed of past abuse from authority. In this chapter, we will look at the positive side. There is a direct relationship between respecting authority and receiving blessings. The rule is this: *respect authority, receive blessing*. As respect goes upward, blessing comes downward.

The Ten Commandments deal with just parental authority. Paul made that rule universal in **Ephesians 5-6**: Not only parental authority, but all the four categories of delegated human authority; not just long life, but all kinds of blessing. Parental authority is the foundation for other types of human authority and that is why it is listed as part of the Ten Commandments.

Ephesians 6:2 "Honor your father and your mother" is the first commandment with a promise.

All blessings originate in God. He passes on those blessings to us in the spirit realm. He created the network of delegated authority to transfer spiritual blessings to us from heaven into the earth. As we pass honor upward, blessings flow downward.

Ephesians 1:3

God... has blessed us with every spiritual blessing in the heavens in Messiah.

We receive all blessings from God through Yeshua. We can receive some of them directly by faith in the spirit. We can also receive them through delegated authority. As we pass honor upward, blessings flow downward. As we submit upward, authority can be delegated downward. (There is a difference between honoring and submitting, which we will deal with in the next chapter.)

To summarize this authority matrix, the principle works in:

- 2 directions (up and down – **Luke 7**)

- 2 types (good and bad – **Deuteronomy 5**)

- 2 realms (heaven and earth – **Matthew 28**)

- 4 categories (family, work, government, church –
  Ephesians 5-6).

In each channel of authority, there is potentially both good and bad which can be passed on.

You can honor your parents and receive family blessings; honor your spiritual parents and receive spiritual blessings. We refer to this as "spiritual inheritance." You might ask why you need to honor spiritual fathers. Why not just get the blessings yourself through prayer and obedience? The answer is that you can indeed get all blessings from prayer and obedience by faith. The benefit of spiritual inheritance is that it can come in much greater ways and much more quickly.

[**Note:** The potential of parental blessing and spiritual blessing together is enormous. Jacob's blessing from Isaac included not only family and material blessings, but a transfer of manifold spiritual authority. **Genesis 27:29** – **"Let peoples serve you, and nations bow down to you. Be master over your brethren, and let your mother's sons bow down to you."**

While this blessing started out small within Jacob's tribe, it increased its spiritual dimensions over the generations until it became the basis for all future kingdom authority. Jacob's blessing will extend all the way to heavenly Jerusalem having 12 gates named after the 12 tribes. Yeshua had 12 disciples in His inner circle and 70 in the second circle, just as Jacob had 12 sons and 70 grandsons. (It even may be considered the basis for every national government in the world today – see **Deuteronomy 32:8**.)]

After coming to faith in the late 1970's, I had difficulty finding my direction to serve the Lord. Since I came to faith in Latin America, I thought perhaps I was called to be an evangelist there. However, after much prayer and fasting, the Lord showed me that the key to finding my destiny lay in honoring my parents. This did not seem logical because neither of my parents were believers at the time.

As I reluctantly agreed to honor my parents, I simply realized that both my **Dad and Mom** were Jewish. The revelation of Messianic Judaism and of my own calling opened up to me. My Mom said to me, "If this is what you want to do, why don't you do it right? Even though I don't agree with you, I will fly you to visit Israel and pay for you to get a degree in theology."

Immediately after that, I began to work for a senior pioneer Messianic evangelist named **Manny Brotman.** I served as his personal assistant for a year in the late 1970's. Through him I had received my first "mandate" or "commission" to serve in the Messianic Jewish movement.

Soon after that I met **Dan Juster,** while I was still a new believer. Dan was known for teaching Jewish roots of the faith. However, Dan also had a broad knowledge of systematic theology, church history and ministry experience that I did not. By my honoring and submitting to him, he was able to direct my studies and impart wisdom that would have taken me many more years to attain, if ever.

Dan and I, together with **Eitan Shishkoff,** started a network of Messianic ministries, known today as Tikkun International. We continue today in a covenantal partnership that has had far-reaching effects.

Although we developed separate spheres of cooperating ministries, Dan has had a special place in my life as primary mentor and spiritual father. In recent years, Dan has come to Israel and joined back together with us in our local team. What a great testimony of long-term faithfulness this has been!

I then served under **Thurlow Switzer** at a Christian high school academy in the mid 1980's and eventually became the principal there. Thurlow came from generations of Baptist pastors and a conservative evangelical background that was totally foreign to me. Through serving under his authority, I gained character values that would have been otherwise inaccessible to me. Much of what I wrote in Covenant Relationships came from his and Dan's mentoring.

When I moved to Israel, there were many pioneers in the Land. **Joseph Shulam** had a profound understanding of "restoring the kingdom to Israel" (**Acts 1:6**). During my first years after Aliyah, I served as Joe's assistant pastor. From him I learned much of Israeli Jewish culture and personality that was new to me. Joseph and I come from very different "streams" theologically. Eventually, we separated our work from one another, yet we did so on good terms. Because I honor his role in the Land, I was able to reap blessings from the Lord through him.

After that I served as assistant to **Ilan Zamir.** Although Ilan was younger than I, he had a unique leadership authority in the Land. Through serving together with him under his leadership, we were able to build the foundations for the Messianic Jewish Alliance of Israel that continues successfully today. When Ilan went on to be with the Lord, **Hanan Lukats** was chosen to be the new president, and the alliance has grown under his leadership. Both of these men had unique qualities that I do not have. By serving with them and recognizing their calling, I have been able to take part in the Alliance leadership which I could not have done on my own.

Ari Sorkoram and I had a very similar vision about building a congregation with a core of local Israelis in the Hebrew language and with the power of the Holy Spirit. Under his leadership, along with pastor **Eddie Santoro,** we worked together to build Tiferet Yeshua congregation in Tel Aviv. After that time, Eddie came with me to start Ahavat Yeshua congregation in Jerusalem.

In 2013 Ari asked me to come back to take the senior leadership oversight of Tiferet. Through honoring both Ari's and Eddie's experience and gifting, we were able to launch the two sister congregations, one in Jerusalem and one in Tel Aviv. After that I worked with **Ron Cantor** to train a new generation of younger disciples to take the leadership in the congregation.

Our base of Revive Israel Ministries is located at Yad Hashmona Messianic kibbutz (moshav). We are not in leadership at the kibbutz, but we support their vision. **Aryeh Bar David** has been a key spiritual father in the growth of the kibbutz. He and the other Israeli pioneers took over from the first Finnish founders. They have spent years of hard labor to build Yad Hashmona. Aryeh is not a spiritual father to me personally. However, because we honor him as a spiritual father in the Land, we receive blessing. We simply recognize their investment and honor them for what they have done. By honoring them, God has opened a wonderful door of opportunity for cooperation between Revive Israel and Yad Hashmona.

Time would run short for me to mention all the spiritual fathers in the land of Israel or for me personally, such as **Victor Smadja, Don Finto** and **David Rudolph.** By honoring spiritual fathers, we receive a spiritual inheritance far beyond our own ability to achieve for ourselves. This allows us to produce enormous fruit for the kingdom of God, while at the same time remaining humble, since we know that the inheritance was just passed on and not accomplished by our own deeds.

Another added benefit is that the spiritual inheritance received can then be easily passed on to others. Today, there are younger disciples that look to me as a spiritual father. I hope to be able to pass on to them all that was given to me by spiritual fathers, so that they can multiply it much further in their generation. (See supplement 10 on "Spiritual Inheritance," by Don Finto and Tod McDowell.) Freely we have received, so freely we can give to others (**Matthew 10:8**).

We have taken this principle so far as to dare to claim by faith that the first-century apostles are our "spiritual fathers" to some degree. As Israeli Messianic Jews, we try to see ourselves as distant relatives of their extended family. Well, why not? We desire to have all of the revival power, holiness, and vision that they had. It's all stored up in heavenly places, waiting for us to inherit it by faith and grace. (See supplement 11 on "Recovering the Apostolic Commission.")

All blessings that we receive by honoring human authority figures are imperfect and partial. However, we can also receive blessings directly from heaven by honoring God Himself through praise and worship.

Revelation 7:12

Blessing and glory and wisdom, thanksgiving, and honor and power and might be to our God forever!

In some ways, worship is honoring God our Father as the ultimate authority figure. As we give God glory and honor going upward, He pours out blessings downward upon us - gloriously, powerfully and eternally. Halleluyah!

QUESTIONS FOR REFLECTION:

What rule describes the relationship between authority and blessing?

What are the three primary benefits of honoring spiritual fathers?

In addition to honoring spiritual fathers, what else must we do to receive the fullness of blessing?

CHAPTER FOURTEEN
RESPONDING TO IMPROPER AUTHORITY

Although there is blessing whenever we honor godly authority, there is also danger in trying to obey unrighteous authority. How are we to respond when authority is being used improperly or sinfully? First, we have to discern between the three levels or ways to respond to authority: Respect, Submission and Obedience. They are not at all the same. The difference between them is critically important.

1. **Respect** – Respect and honor are the same. We are to honor and respect all legitimate forms of authority because they are under the overall sovereignty of God. We are honoring the One from whom all authority flows, regardless of the human beings who are in the positions of authority.

2. **Submit** – Submission is the attitude of recognizing someone else's authority over you. It

is to place yourself under that person's authority. While we honor all authority, we only submit to authority when we are in that person's sphere of authority. Sometimes we have a choice as to whether to place ourselves in someone's sphere of authority; sometimes we do not have a choice.

3. **Obey** – To obey is to do and act according to what the person in authority says. We honor all authority. We submit to authority when we are positioned in that sphere of authority. We obey authority that we are submitted to as long as we are not asked to sin or violate one of God's absolute moral standards.

All three dimensions of responding to authority require wisdom, faith and humility.

Here are simplified guidelines for responding to authority in right or wrong situations:

- If the authority we are submitted to makes a right decision, we obey.

- If the authority we are submitted to makes an unwise decision, but not sinful, we still obey. (In this case you think it would have been better for the authority to take a different course, but the decision was nevertheless within reasonable or conceivable options. So you should choose to cooperate.)

- Sometimes the authority makes a decision that is not only unwise but wrong. It may not be sinful or evil, but it is worse than just unwise. What makes it wrong is that people will be hurt by the results. If the authority we are submitted to makes a wrong decision, we can obey, but we should appeal the decision and ask the authority to consider changing it.

- If the authority we are submitted to makes an evil or sinful decision, we must disobey, but maintain an attitude of submission and honor. (In this case the authority has crossed a line of moral violation. We cannot obey. We make no effort to rebel against the whole authority, but we clearly refuse to obey, while being respectful in attitude.) You never have to submit to sin. "Submission ends where sin begins."

- If we are submitted to an authority that is not right for us, and we have the option to change spheres of authority, we should change. (You do not always have to stay in a situation that is abusive. Sometimes there is the option to leave.)

- If we are relating to an authority sphere that we are not part of, we should act with respect but not submission or obedience.

These principles create a ladder of respect-submission-obedience:

1. Not your sphere: Honor without submission

2. Your sphere: Honor and submit

3. Your sphere with good decision: Honor, submit and obey

4. Your sphere with unwise decision: Honor, submit and obey

5. Your sphere with wrong decision: Honor, submit, obey and appeal

6. Your sphere with sinful decision: Honor with submissive heart, yet disobey

7. Wrong sphere: Honor, yet switch spheres if you have the opportunity.

Lastly, there are numerous and various situations where one must submit and suffer. In that case there is need for a special impartation of the grace and power of God.

Let's look at some examples, both modern and biblical.

Romans 13:1

Let every soul be subject to governing authorities. There is no authority except from God, and the authorities that exist are appointed by God.

I Peter 2:13

Submit yourselves to every institution of man for the Lord's sake

The apostles told us that all authority is from God. This reflects the world view of the Israelite prophets of the sovereignty of God. He appoints people into positions of authority according to His will and He removes them (**Daniel 4:17, 25, 32**). There are multiple levels of authority, and God is above them all (**Ecclesiastes 5:8**). He will hold them accountable for their actions, yet He takes responsibility for the fact that they hold those positions.

Regardless of what we think about those in authority, we should see them as mere instruments in the hands of an almighty

God. Paul's and Peter's exhortation to "submit to all governing authorities" is an application and extension of Yeshua's statement that "all authority in heaven and on earth" was given to Him.

To accept the sovereign hand of God over the governing powers demands extraordinary degrees of both faith and humility. Those in authority often do wrong. How can that situation be according to the will of God? At one point Yeshua addressed the problem of accepting the sovereignty of God when Pilate mixed the blood of Galilean citizens in the blood of sacrifices (**Luke 13:1-2**).

In the verses above, the apostles are referring to a situation in which you are part of a certain institution or authority sphere. Yet Peter himself, while being respectful and submissive, totally refused to obey people or institutions that made a sinful decision, as in the case of the Sanhedrin arresting them for sharing the gospel:

Acts 4:19

Whether it is right in the sight of God to listen to you more than to God, you judge.

Acts 5:29

We ought to obey God rather than man.

In this case, the commission to preach the gospel was above the authority of the Sanhedrin. So the apostles disobeyed. When human authority breaks a direct command of divine authority, we have no choice but to disobey. The higher authority overrules the lower authority.

When Paul rebuked the high priest, he tried to maintain an attitude of respect (**Acts 23:5**). Yet when he realized he would never receive justice from them, he decided to switch judicial authority spheres by turning to the high court in Rome (**Acts**

25:11). This is a case of changing authority spheres if necessary and possible. Paul had this opportunity because he was a Roman citizen, whereas Peter and the others were not.

Yeshua did not fight the soldiers who came to arrest Him and spoke respectfully to Pilate, although He did not stop His mission or message (**John 18:11; 19:11**). Yeshua appealed to the high priest to change after they struck Him (**John 18:23**). Yeshua did not even answer the priests' questions until they exercised their authority and "foreswore" Him to answer (**Matthew 26:63**).

A woman should not marry a man who is not a believer for that would put her under a wrong authority. Once she is married, she cannot change husbands. If the husband is an unbeliever and wants to leave, she has the option of being released from that authority (**I Corinthians 7:10-15**). If the husband breaks the covenant of marriage (such as by adultery), then she may have the option of being released as well.

If her husband tells her to commit adultery, she must obviously disobey. If her husband makes a wrong decision, she may ask him to reconsider. Even Pilate's wife asked him to reconsider his decision concerning Yeshua (**Matthew 27:19**).

When Yoseph and Miriam (Yeshua's parents) realized that the government's soldiers were hunting to kill Yeshua, they simply left the country to another jurisdiction according to an angel's instruction (**Matthew 2:13**). Yeshua as an adult during His ministry decided to spend most of His time in the Galilee because the antagonistic religious leaders in Judah wanted to kill Him (**John 7:1**). He did not just stay there and allow Himself to be killed. He moved to another jurisdiction.

When Yeshua was a teenager, He felt the conflict between heavenly and earthly authority. He did tell His parents that He had decided to stay in Jerusalem to study Torah for a few more days because that was His heavenly Father's "business" (**Luke 2:49**). But then He returned home and submitted to His earthly father's "business" (**Luke 2:51**). It would seem that because of the balance of following His own calling from the heavenly Father, yet submitting temporarily to His earthly father, Yeshua was able to grow in wisdom and favor both with God and men (**Luke 2:52**).

Modern Israel has a difficult relationship with Turkey. The government had been moderately Muslim for years but has been turning more radically Muslim recently. There are many issues with which Turkey and Israel are in conflict. Often they are engaged in petty diplomatic games of insulting one another, which has no real advantage to either but only makes the practical issues harder. From the biblical worldview, even if a people are your enemy, and even if you have to go to war against them, you should still treat them with honor.

When Joshua and the children of Israel conquered the land of Canaan, they were executing a judgment of God in war that included the death penalty for the seven nations living there (**Deuteronomy 7:1**). They executed that death penalty and as deterrence even hanged their leaders on trees or wooden poles. Yet at the same time they made sure to lower them and bury them so as not to disgrace God's image in them (**Joshua 8:29; 10:26-27**).

This was in accord with the Torah which allowed death penalty but demanded human respect at the same time (**Deuteronomy 21:22-23**). The law of the Torah was in direct contrast to the pagan Philistines who kept the bodies of King Saul and Jonathan hanging and shamefully exposed in Bet Shean until the Israelites of Jabesh Gilead came to remove and bury them (**I Samuel 31:9-13**). The death penalty may at times be a necessary form of punishment, yet desecration of body never is.

David served under King Saul for a period. Saul became jealous and tried to kill him. Through Jonathan (Saul's son and David's friend), David tried to appeal to Saul to change his attitude. Finally, David saw that Saul would not change. Therefore, he decided to leave. He could no longer stay under Saul's authority. He switched spheres and went to serve the Philistine king, Achish in Gat (**I Samuel 27:1-2**). Even though Achish was pagan, he had a higher moral standard. It was better for David to switch authority spheres than to stay submitted to Saul and be destroyed.

Jonathan in my opinion made a tragic mistake. He was caught between honoring his father's parental and kingly authority on the one hand, and David's divine messianic anointing on the other hand. Had his dad only made unwise or even wrong decisions, Jonathan would have been correct to stay. However, Saul tried to murder David; he crossed the line. He made evil and sinful decisions that violated the absolute moral standards of God. At that point Jonathan should have left him to go with David.

When Ariel Sharon was an opposition leader and a cabinet member in Israel, he was known for his strong right wing positions. When he became prime minister, he moderated that stance. When questioned, he replied, "What you see from here is not what you see from there." When he had the responsibility to make the final decision that would affect everyone and when he had all the information from the different sides of the issue available to him, he had to use his authority in a different way.

Some believers find themselves in congregations where the pastor or senior leader is abusive. They have to use discernment and make a decision as to which response is appropriate. They may decide to stay and submit; to stay and appeal; to stay and disobey; or to leave. All those could potentially be correct options depending on the situation.

If the decision is to stay, then respect and submission should be maintained. If an appeal is brought, then it should be with a heart of respect through principles of covenantal confrontation. However, we also have the option to leave. Part of abusive leadership is to manipulate and pressure the flock so that they cannot leave. Being pressured to stay under spiritual leadership that is abusive is symptomatic of a cult. There is no biblical imperative to remain in such a situation.

Yeshua said that we may be in a position where someone slaps us on the face. For the sake of witnessing the grace of God and victorious faith, we should offer them the other cheek (**Matthew 5:39**). However, that is not the same issue as submitting to abusive pastoral leadership. In that case, Paul told us just the opposite.

II Corinthians 11:20

For you put up with it if one brings you into bondage, if one devours you, if one takes from you... if one strikes you on the face.

Paul is rebuking the church in Corinth for putting up with abusive leaders. That is not godly, nor is it what Yeshua intended. There is a difference between overcoming a slap in the face to demonstrate grace and putting up with being slapped continually by abusive leadership. A believer is not required to stay in a congregation where he is being abused.

Likewise, a wife is not required to be abused. Depending on the level of abuse, whether psychological or physical, whether repeated or occasional, the wife must decide on the proper course of action. She should remain respectful but does not have to be abused. There are a variety of options from pastoral counseling to police intervention. Discernment is needed according to each individual situation.

Sometimes, however, God does lead us to stay and suffer. When Hagar fled from Sarah's anger, the Angel of the Lord told her to return even though she would have to suffer (**Genesis 16:9**). Sometimes suffering under authority has a greater kingdom benefit that is hidden from our eyes. But that kind of situation should have a specific leading from the Lord to put up with it.

Many times in life, however, we find ourselves in situations of suffering and there is no option to leave. Suffering is often connected specifically to submission to abusive or even evil authorities. In any kind of suffering in any kind of situation, we can always turn to the Lord to find special grace.

I Peter 2:21

For to this you were called, because Messiah also suffered for us, leaving us an example, that you should follow in his footsteps.

In the situations of needing to suffer through submission to abusive authority, we are taking up our cross as Yeshua did, and a special impartation of the glory of God will come upon us (**I Peter 4:14**). Suffering at the hands of evil men can always be turned to good if we respond in faith to develop in us deeper qualities of patience, godliness and Christ-likeness (**Romans 8:17-18, 28, II Corinthians 1:7, Philippians 1:29; 3:10, James 1:3, I Peter 1:6-7; 2:18-23; 3:14-17; 4:1, 12-16; 5:9-10**).

Suffering at the hands of evil men or abusive authority has been a common, almost universal experience of righteous men and women around the world throughout history. (The issue of the relationship between suffering and glory is a vast subject, worthy of a separate volume or two in itself, which hopefully we can approach in another book altogether.)

Christians in the underground church in China suffered greatly for their faith at the hands of an ungodly and persecuting government. Special grace and power was upon them. Out of their suffering arose the greatest sweep of evangelism in history with over 100 million people coming to faith. Supernatural miracles were daily experiences in the midst of their harsh suffering.

Today there are brave saints in underground churches in the midst of the world of Islamic Jihad. We must pray for strength for these dear brothers and sisters, and at the same time fight to end the horrible injustices in Muslim-controlled nations.

In the underground churches in the Communist or Muslim world, there were a variety of attitudes by faith as to how to react to the governing authorities. In all cases, the believers looked for the greater opportunities to bring salvation to their people. Let us continue to pray for all people who have to suffer for their faith.

Scriptures are filled with examples of righteous people responding to ungodly authority. We can think of Joseph before Potiphar; Moses before Pharaoh; Jeremiah before Zedekiah; Daniel before Nebuchadnezzar; Mordecai before Haman, and so on. Let us learn from their examples of how to respect authority and stand for integrity at the same time.

QUESTIONS FOR REFLECTION:

What are the three ways to respond to authority?

Describe the different contexts for Yeshua's comments about "turning the other cheek" and Paul's encouragement to flee from abusive leadership?

What should accompany any continued submission to abusive or evil authority?

CHAPTER 15
DISCIPLESHIP AND EQUIPPING

There is a profound connection between discipleship for a believer in Yeshua and dealing with issues of delegated authority. Notice again the connection between authority (**verse 18**) and discipleship (**verse 19**) in the Great Commission. "All authority" leads to "make disciples."

Matthew 28:18-20

All authority has been given to me in heaven and on earth. Go therefore and make disciples of all the nations, baptizing them in the name of the Father and of the Son and of the Holy Spirit, teaching them to observe all things that I have commanded you, and behold, I am with you always.

In this context, the position of Yeshua as Messiah is one of a king with authority. He has spiritual authority in heaven. The message of the gospel is to proclaim that His authority in heaven is in the process of repossessing planet earth. The inhabitants of earth are given a chance to submit to His authority. Immersion in water (baptism) is not only a sign of forgiveness of sins, but of submitting to King Messiah and His heavenly authority. (See Supplement12: "Gospel of the Kingdom.")

We are to make disciples, which is to teach people how to live according to Yeshua's heavenly authority and His earthly authority. We must learn how to relate to both direct and delegated authority. Notice that Yeshua's teachings are called here "commandments." The teachings of Yeshua are just as much a commandment in the New Covenant as the Ten Commandments were in the Torah. [See the section on "Yeshua and the Torah" in the book "Who Ate Lunch with Abraham?"]

In **verse 20**, we are instructed to teach others to "observe all." To observe means to obey. Discipleship is to teach people to obey Yeshua's teachings. The New Covenant demands obedience to Yeshua's commandments as the Torah demanded obedience to its commandments.

[**Note:** In fact we are to keep all of the commandments of the Torah (**Matt. 5:17**), not the traditions of men (**Matt. 15:3**), in the way taught to us by our great Rabbi Yeshua (**Matt. 19:16-19**), and His Apostles; being led by God's Spirit (**Romans 8:4**) with the commandments written on our hearts through the New Covenant (**Jeremiah 31:33**). The question is not *whether* we keep the commandments but *how.*]

Paul's teaching about salvation by grace and righteousness by faith includes obedience:

Romans 1:5

...obedience by faith for all nations.

Romans 6:16

... obedience that leads to righteousness.

Romans 16:26

...bring the nations to obedience.

The gospel includes the declaration of Yeshua's lordship. Baptism (immersion) includes submission to His authority. Discipleship is teaching how to obey and "observe." In addition to learning how to tell others about salvation (evangelism), discipleship has four major parts:

1. **Personal relationships** – meeting regularly with a person more mature in faith for heart discussions of personal spiritual growth as part of a community of fellow believers.

2. **Study** – developing a habit of daily Scripture meditation along with reading other material for strengthening our faith.

3. **Experiencing the Holy Spirit** – actively participating in regular times of prayer and worship, privately or in a group setting, in which the gifts of the Spirit are working and the presence of the Holy Spirit brings healing and correction.

4. **Practical service** – doing small chores or acts of service with accountability and follow-up with clearly-defined submission to authority.

Discipleship should be done with someone who has a measure of spiritual fruit and maturity whom you can trust. Counseling, Scripture study, and operation in the gifts of the Holy Spirit all need to have a mentor-coach authority figure involved. Doing practical service with clear job descriptions under a person in charge develops humility and a submissive heart.

I have seen this carried out so well with our friends at *Gateways Beyond Training Schools* in Cyprus and other locations around the world. They use a regime of daily practical chores to identify character issues and "problems with authority." One can "fake" being spiritual in the first 3 areas of discipleship, but when asked to do practical service under supervision, the character issues rise quickly to the surface.

The most basic fruit of discipleship should be daily devotional times and active participation in a local congregation. If that occurs, the person will likely remain stable and fruitful as a well-watered tree (**Psalm 1:1-3**). The goal is for a person to be a stable and fruitful believer walking with Yeshua in grace, faith and obedience.

You might be a young person (or older for that matter) who is looking for someone to disciple you and just cannot find anyone. Perhaps there is no discipleship school available for you. What can be done? In some ways, the "disciplee" has to be more pro-active than the "discipler." This may not be the ideal, but often is the reality.

You may have to initiate your own discipleship situation. Find fellowship; ask to meet with a mature believer; read books; develop a daily Bible meditation habit; seek to submit and serve someone; participate in prayer and praise meetings; go out to talk about Yeshua to someone who does not yet know Him. Do whatever it takes.

We started the Revive Israel ministry team in 2003 with a group of 12 young Israeli disciples. We tried to pattern ourselves after Yeshua and the Twelve. The question arose as to what was their basic role. Were they Yeshua's:

1. Students?

2. Staff?

3. Future leaders in training?

The answer obviously was: **all three.** There were times to learn, times to serve in basic chores, and times to be involved in the ministry with Yeshua.

In the gospels, the followers of Yeshua are called *disciples*, never *saints.* In the epistles, they are called *saints* not *disciples.* In the book of Acts, in between, they are called by both terms (apparently a transition).

In the gospels, we are called to "make" or "teach" disciples (**Matthew 28:19**). In the epistles we are called to "equip" the saints.

Ephesians 4:12

...equipping the saints for the work of ministry.

It seems there are three over-lapping stages of development.

1. Salvation

2. Discipleship

3. Equipping

The words for salvation in both Hebrew and Greek include the ideas of healing, deliverance, protection and being made "whole." A person is made whole as he accepts forgiveness of sins, eternal life, and comes into the kingdom of God. The inner healing and wholeness of salvation is a process that continues long after a person first receives Yeshua as lord and savior.

The word for discipleship in Greek is the same as the root for "mathematics." There is a program of "formation" that has structure and systematic principles. The word disciple also contains the concept of "discipline." In Hebrew the word for making disciples means to learn and also to make someone "stand up." When a person can stand stable in faith, he is fulfilling his program of discipleship. While discipleship can be a definite program which can be accomplished in a short period of time, it is also a process that lasts our whole lives.

Equipping is less systematic than discipleship. It has to do with bringing each person into their God-given destiny. It is based on gifts and callings of the Holy Spirit. It brings a person to serve in ministry. It trains the saint for leadership (more on this in the following chapter). While discipleship deals much with submission to authority, equipping continues the process to learn how to exercise and delegate authority.

It saddens me to note that such a large number of leaders today never themselves had to submit to someone else's authority, to serve someone else's vision or to go through a process of discipleship themselves. Many were never healed of basic emotional and psychological wounds. If someone tries to lead others when he himself has not been led by others, there are many problems and complications that ensue.

Before a person can develop his own vision, he must "**serve someone else's vision**." Yeshua said that if we can serve in something insignificant and temporary, which belongs to someone else, then we can have what is significant and eternal, which belongs to us. Who would want to serve you if you have never served someone else?

Matthew 25:21

You were faithful over a few things, I will make you ruler over many things.

Luke 16:12

If you were not faithful in what is another man's, who will give you what is your own?

In the modern Messianic Jewish, charismatic or evangelical worlds, there is a certain pride connected to what someone's "ministry" is. Do you know what the word for "ministry" is in Hebrew? Well, there isn't one. The only way to say it is **"sherut"** שרות , which is the same word for a taxi, a lavatory, or room service. It just means "serving." Being in ministry, serving someone else's vision and cleaning a toilet are similar to one another.

QUESTIONS FOR REFLECTION:

What is the primary goal of discipleship?

What are the four primary parts of discipleship?

What are the three stages of faith development for followers of Yeshua?

Why is it important for all leaders in the Body of Messiah to begin in submission to someone else?

CHAPTER 16
LESSONS IN LEADERSHIP

Every person has a destiny in Yeshua. That destiny has two aspects: a universal aspect that is common to every believer in the world, and a specific destiny that is particular and fitting only to that person's soul and personality.

Romans 8:29-30

For whom God foreknew, he also predestined to be conformed to the image of his Son, that he might be the firstborn among many brethren. Moreover, whom he predestined he also called; whom he called, these he justified, and whom he justified he also glorified.

There are five stages of development here: foreknew, predestined, called, justified and glorified. It is like the process of a caterpillar turning into a butterfly. [For a fuller description of these stages, see our book "*The Apple of His Eye*."] God knows our soul better than we know ourselves, and He designs a plan perfectly suited just for us and no one else. That is our specific destiny.

However, our universal destiny is "to be conformed to the image of his Son." God's plan for each and every one of us is to become "just like Jesus;" to be "Christ-like;" to be remade into the image of God. That is the goal of discipleship (actually the same goal of creation in which we were made in God's image). Moving on to our specific destiny is the process of equipping.

Ephesians 4:12

... equipping the saints for the work of ministry.

Equipping is training: for career and calling; for divine destiny; and for spiritual vocation and leadership.

Ironically, the first part of leadership training is to be broken; broken totally of every thought that you can accomplish something on your own ability. All the great men of God go through this process.

Abraham had the calling to be the best father in the whole world. He is the father of every man or woman of faith. God knew Abraham's soul and his desire to be a dad. God had him wait childless for 100 years until he felt totally hopeless (**Romans 4:16-21**).

Jacob became so desperately disgusted with his own manipulative and cowardly personality that he "wrestled with God" all night. God's solution for the root of the problem was to change his name and change his very identity from Jacob (a heel grabber) to Israel (a prince with God) - **Genesis 32:24-28**.

Joseph, a natural born leader, had to stay in jail for years until his pride was broken (**Genesis 39:20-41:14**).

Moses, perhaps the most talented and gifted leader of all time, had to be humbled in the wilderness 40 years until he begged God to choose someone else (**Exodus 3:11**).

David's lies, adultery and murder were exposed to the whole nation and written in the Bible. David's depth of repentance is also recorded. He begged God not to take the Holy Spirit from him (**Psalm 51:11**) and to receive the sacrifices of his broken and contrite heart (**Psalm 51:17**).

Peter reached a unique level of leadership and spiritual power. He was the head of the early community of disciples, had keys of spiritual authority in heaven and on earth, preached to thousands in Jerusalem, and even raised the dead. People laid the sick in the streets so that his shadow alone would heal them (**Acts 5:15**). Even Yeshua was not recorded as doing such healings. The only way someone could get to such a height of spiritual power is to go to the depth of spiritual humility and repentance.

Yeshua told Peter that he would be attacked by the devil, but He only prayed for his faith to be restored afterwards (**Luke 22:32**). Yeshua announced that Peter would deny him three times on the same night (**verse 34**). It was from the depths of that brokenness that Peter would return to do so many miracles and lead the early church into revival. Peter had become so humble that when he wrote his epistles in the New Testament, he did not even mention the great miracles that God had done through him.

No person helped spread the gospel and influence history more than Paul. Yet Paul was bitterly distressed at his own sinfulness. He called himself "the worst of sinners" (**I Timothy 1:15**). Paul knew that he had persecuted the saints of God. At the Damascus road experience, Paul was blinded for three days. He fasted and prayed. I believe God showed him hell and the fires of punishment that Paul was already condemned to. Only by the grace of God would he be able to live. The fear of God and the despising of his own flesh were part of Paul's unwavering devotion and zeal.

To be fully used of God, we must have our selfishness and self-centeredness removed. That can be a painful process. Often the only way we can reach our full calling and character development is to go through something that seems just the opposite of our gifting. The road to destiny is filled with adversity. (See Supplement 13: "Walking through Adversity" by Phil Wagler.)

- Moses was raised as crown prince of Egypt, and God used him to punish Egypt and take the Israelites out into the wilderness.

- David was a shepherd boy, and God raised him to be king of Israel.

- Jonah's background was pro-Zionist and nationalist, prophesying military expansion for Israel (**II Kings 14:25**). Yet God used him to bring revival to Israel's enemy Assyria.

- Peter, the blundering, uneducated Galilean fisherman, was used to confront the great Jewish religious leaders in Jerusalem and call them to repentance.

- Paul, the genius rabbinical student and ultra-Orthodox Jew, was used to found the churches among the Gentiles.

Training to be a leader in God's kingdom is quite the opposite of what we might think. Since God is all-powerful and since men tend to be treacherous, God is looking to train us in humility, faithfulness, compassion and patience much more than He is looking for people who are gifted in order to develop their talents. Every talent or ability that a man has is the potential place of his downfall or success.

There seems to be a perfectly balanced measure that to the degree that God will use a person in power and authority, the person needs to be broken of pride. To the degree that God will raise someone up, he has to lower the person down. (See Supplement 14: "High and Low," by David Block.)

Two of the greatest generals of the Bible were Joshua and Joab. Joshua conquered the land of Israel; Joab conquered Jerusalem and led David's mighty army. Joab was such an intensely focused warrior that he often thought David was too soft or lenient. Joab eventually betrayed David at the end of his life. Joshua, on the other hand, submitted to Moses's spiritual rebukes (**Numbers 11:29**) and spent much time in prayer (**Exodus 33:11**) in order to balance his warrior side.

Two men in David's time had a great gift of wise counsel: Hushai, David's friend, and Ahitophel, who became counselor for Absalom. For Hushai, his gift of counsel was less important than his friendship to David. Ahitophel, in contrast, was desirous for people to appreciate his gift of counsel. Eventually, God caused Hushai's advice to be accepted rather than Ahitophel's. In response, Ahitophel committed suicide. People who have a gift of counsel may sometimes become extremely offended when their advice is not heeded.

For many people, expressing their gifts and talents is the most important thing in life. If their gift is not used and recognized, they are traumatized. Their identity gets so caught up with their talent that, like a drug, they cannot live without it.

The name Absalom (Avshalom) is of the same root as Solomon (Shlomo), meaning peace (shalom). Avshalom and Shlomo were both crown princes and heirs to the throne of David. Avshalom had a gift to attract people; he was a people "magnet." Instead of keeping his ability submitted to David's authority, Absalom drew people away from David. He did not respect David as his father, or David's authority as king. He found pleasure in people's attention. (See supplement 15, on "Don't Touch the Bride.")

Those who have the ability to attract people must be careful not to let that gift lead them to rebel against authority like Absalom.

There were two priests in the time of David: Abiathar and Zadok. They went through all of the hardships together with him. There is nothing written that points to any major difference between them. However, at the end of David's life, Zadok stayed loyal to him, whereas Abiathar betrayed him along with Adonijah and Joab. Two people can be serving alongside one another in a similar way, yet one can be developing more and more loyalty, while the other harbors resentment. Let us guard our hearts over the long run to stay faithful to the end.

Even Yeshua went through a transition to receive the anointing and authority from the leader before Him. In this case it was His own cousin Yohanan (John the Baptist), who happened to be only three months older than He was. The transition went through 3 stages:

1. Submission to the previous leader

2. Continuance of the same message

3. New creativity and advancement.

Yeshua came to John and asked to be immersed in water by him. That was to recognize John's spiritual authority as a prophet (**Matthew 3:15**). Then Yeshua went out to preach the same message that John preached concerning repentance (**Matthew 3:1-2, 4:17**). After a period of continuing in John's footsteps, Yeshua added His new dimension of believing in the good news of salvation (**Mark 1:15**). If Yeshua could follow this three-fold process of leadership transition, how much more can we!

The point in all these examples is that a loyal, submissive and serving heart is more important in the long run than any strength or ability. As part of God's training, He often brings us to a place of humility and brokenness before He blesses us with power and authority. God's training is the opposite of those who seek success in the eyes of men. Let's embrace His character development in our lives, no matter how painful or humiliating it may seem for the time being.

QUESTIONS FOR REFLECTION:

What are the five stages of the development of a person's destiny in Yeshua according to Romans 8:29-30?

What is the destiny of every follower of Yeshua?

What is a person being equipped to do in Ephesians 4:12?

What is the first part of eldership training?

What is more important than strength and ability in a leader?

CHAPTER 17
KING DAVID'S EXAMPLE

Most of the historical books of the Bible, particularly Samuel, Kings and Chronicles, describe the effort to establish the throne of David. This throne represents the head of delegated divine authority on earth – and so the stakes are extremely high. As a result, there was tremendous struggle and sin in the lives of those men and women involved in these "throne games." Their stories recorded in the Bible provide a handbook on "how and how not" to respond to authority.

In the Torah we find Joshua submitted to and serving Moses. He did this for many years. We also find him with a deep personal devotional life of intimacy with YHVH himself. He literally stayed in the tabernacle (**Exodus 33:11**). The book of Joshua tells of the conquest of the land of Canaan and also of Joshua's leadership.

So Joshua had devotional purity, submission to authority, and clear delegation of authority. His leadership produced great victory in his generation and in the generation following (**Josh.**

24:31). Thus the historical books actually started off with great success.

However, by the time we get to the book of Judges, the situation has deteriorated. The first area of problem was the people not wanting any leadership at all. The thought of the people was "no one is going to tell me what to do." The recurring theme of the book of Judges is that **"In those days there was no king in Israel; everyone did what was right in his own eyes" – Judges 21:25.**

Many people today use the excuse of "following the Lord" to justify simply doing what they want to do. Such independence causes lack of united cooperation. That attitude can hinder progress in the kingdom of God for several generations to come.

The next spiritual leader was the prophet Samuel. His primary influence was by positive spiritual and moral example. He was known throughout the whole land for his integrity (**I Samuel 12:4**). Although he did not succeed in developing a government or an authority structure, the nation prospered during his time of prophetic leadership.

After that came a tragic mistake: the people wanted a king based on political power and human talent (**I Samuel 8:5**). This was a rejection of God's direct spiritual authority (**I Samuel 8:7**). Saul was chosen as king. There was some success and blessing during his reign; however, there were also problems.

Because the desire for a king was primarily politically and popularly based, there was an inherent disregard for the spiritual side – the priesthood and prophetic ministries. Saul himself began to offer sacrifices, which was a deprecation of Samuel's role and a desire to be honored by the people (**I Samuel 15:30**). Basing leadership on popular opinion or on the desire to be honored by people will eventually lead to disaster.

Then came another unique leader and one of the great heroes of the Bible. God saw certain good qualities in the heart of young boy named David (**I Samuel 16:1, 7, 13**). Like Joshua, David loved to spend personal time worshipping and praising God alone. This time instead of the tabernacle in the wilderness, it was in the field with his sheep. He had moral courage, first against the lion and the bear, and afterwards against Goliath and the enemies of Israel. He was willing to serve under the authority of King Saul and also to take authority in the army with the soldiers under him.

Above all David was known to be a man of moral integrity. The Bible even records that he always did what was right "**except in the case of Uriah the Hittite**" – **I Kings 15:5.** Moral character and godliness are the biblical qualifications for leadership and authority.

While David was still serving Saul, Saul became jealous. The jealousy began to eat away at his heart until he became psychotic and murderous when he thought about David. This caused a dilemma for David. He knew he had a divine destiny to become the king after Saul. Therefore, he wanted in everything to submit to Saul and show him honor. On the other hand, Saul was trying to murder him. Should he submit to evil authority? Should he rebel? Should he flee?

Since David believed in divine sovereignty over Saul, rebellion was not an option for him. He submitted to Saul and honored him even in the midst of the assassination attempts. David even felt guilty once for cutting off the hem of Saul's garment while Saul was in pursuit to murder him (**I Samuel 24:5**). This may be the most extreme example of honoring authority even while the authority is evil.

On the other hand, let us note that David did not stay under Saul's authority for long. He chose to flee, even to the enemy

Philistines. He chose to remove himself from the ungodly authority of Saul. David saw the position of authority of King Saul as divinely ordained, but the use of that authority to be totally evil. Therefore he made the spiritually logical decision to:

1. Remove himself from Saul's sphere of authority

2. Continue to honor Saul because of the position he held

3. Demand divine justice by supernatural intervention when the test would finish

While David humiliated himself before Saul in order to honor him even in the worst moments, he also confronted him and told him that God was going to judge him and punish him for his evil ways. **"May YHVH judge between you and me; and may YHVH avenge me of you; but my hand will not be upon you" – I Samuel 24:12.** While David did not take revenge on his own, he was not just suffering passively. He sought personal physical safety, challenged Saul by moral confrontation, and actively demanded justice from God in prayer.

When David became king, he was righteous in his use of authority. He succumbed to lust and comfort in his affair with Bat Sheva (**II Samuel 11:1-4**) and to pride in the national census for wanting to show that he had more people under him than Moses (**II Samuel 24:1**). In both cases he was extremely repentant; yet, both cases of sin and misuse of authority created damage that lasted for generations.

When David's son Solomon became king he had great wisdom. He took all of David's plans from God and carried them into the next stage of kingdom development. When Solomon could have used his authority for pride and selfishness, he chose instead to ask for wisdom. This was not just the general wisdom to write the Proverbs and Song of Songs, but specific wisdom to use his authority to govern the people with justice and righteousness.

He prayed, **"Give to Your servant a heart to hear how to judge Your people and to understand between good and evil; for who can judge this Your weighty people"** – I Kings 3:9. The word here to "judge" means to make judicial and legislative decisions. While this was a spiritual prayer, the wisdom asked for was to use government authority correctly. So Solomon, like David, chose to submit to authority, to use authority righteously, and to love the Lord personally (**I Kings 3:3**).

Unfortunately, like David, he also sinned in sexual immorality when he was older and had comfort and prosperity (**I Kings 11**). This also caused damage for generations. But because of David and Solomon's overall godliness and righteousness, the governmental aspects of the kingdom of God reached a peak in their generation that was never repeated. (So much so, that even Yeshua's disciples asked Him if He would restore David and Solomon's kingdom – **Acts 1:6**. [See also **Micah 4:8**.])

The example of David before he became king is a wonderful lesson for us all as to how to deal with unrighteous authority, to maintain a submissive heart in the midst of persecution, to turn every attack into an opportunity for character development.

The example of David after he became king is a wonderful lesson for us all as to how to deal with people who are reacting to us in an unrighteous manner when we are in a position of authority and how to make the right decision for the benefit of the kingdom of God instead of our personal gain.

To complete this series of examples, let us look at Solomon's son Rekhav'am (Rehoboam). Rehoboam's misuse of authority is one of the more tragic in the Bible. He had enormous power as Solomon's son. He had a choice to use that authority to be sensitive to the people's needs or to exploit them for his own good.

Rehoboam took counsel from two sets of people; one was the group of senior advisors and the other was the young men who were his colleagues (**I Kings 12:6-8**). The mature counselors advised him to use his power to serve the people and in that way gain their submission and loyalty in a godly way. This was excellent advice and would have maintained the kingdom of God in his day.

The immature counselors advised him to treat the people arrogantly and cruelly and in that way force them into submission whether they liked it or not. This advice was ungodly and ended up splitting the kingdom in two and caused damage that to some extent has not been repaired until this very day.

Not only was the advice ungodly, it was a sign of immaturity. When a person receives authority without being mature, he becomes arrogant and overly self-confident. He thinks of his own power instead of the good of the people. Wisdom over years shows us that leaders do make many mistakes, and therefore, we need to approach leadership decisions with humility and patience.

Immaturity treats humility and patience as weakness, but experience shows that self-restraint is stronger than power (**Proverbs 16:32**). Wisdom and experience know that human beings tend to be selfish and that power tends to corrupt. Therefore, the more one receives authority, the more he should be circumspect; show deference; be quick to listen; and by the fear of God know that he himself could fall easily into pride if not vigilant to maintain humility.

May we learn from these examples of David and the other men from the Scriptures to discern what they did right and what they did wrong. We need to see how they used authority correctly or how they misused authority; and, how they reacted correctly to others' authority, whether good or bad.

QUESTIONS FOR REFLECTION

What is the first spiritual quality for a potential leader that we see in Joshua, Samuel, David and Solomon?

What character flaws made Saul turn bad?

How did David react to Saul when Saul turned against him?

Why did Solomon ask for wisdom?

What was the mistake of immature leadership in Rehoboam?

CHAPTER 18
RESOLVING CONFLICTS

The early community of disciples came to a crisis concerning the standing of Jews and Gentiles in the Body of Messiah. The way in which the conflict was resolved provides a model of how to make decisions in congregations and leadership teams. The process for coming to the right decision was made up of three elements:

1. **Group Discussion – Acts 15:7 - "After there had been much dispute."** The discussion was long and at times heated. Each of the key leaders had a chance to express himself. This is a time-consuming and uncomfortable process. However, if we want to understand God's will, we have to be willing to hear other people's viewpoints. We cannot be afraid of heated discussions.

2. **Holy Spirit Discernment – Acts 15:28 - "For it seemed good to the Holy Spirit and to us."** The personal presence of the Holy Spirit in their midst was seen as a full participant in the discussion,

with His own opinion and will. The disciples made an effort through prayer and fasting (**Acts 13:2**) to listen and submit to the leading of the Holy Spirit.

3. **Leader's Decision – Acts 15:19** - The apostle Jacob (James), as leader of the group declared, **"Therefore I make judgment that..."** His statement reflects the role in Jewish religious courts of the head judge who serves as "posek," the one who renders the final decision. Despite all the open discussion, everyone recognized that at the end there had to be one leader in the group (although he was obviously in mutual accountability with the lead apostles Peter and John).

All three of these elements are needed. The group discussion lets everyone be heard on an equal level. Praying has everyone seeking to hear what God is saying on the issue. The leadership's decision within a clear authority structure allows the group to act decisively once the conclusion is reached.

If there is no group discussion but only the leader (as dynamic as he may be) deciding according to how he hears or believes is right, the sense of teamwork will suffer greatly. There will be no accountability. Potential new leaders will leave in frustration. Valuable differing perspectives will be missed. Even if a leader is certain of the direction the group must take, if he does not involve others in the process of making the decision, they will feel offended and the unity will break down.

If there is no clear leader whose authority is recognized, the group will degenerate into endless analyses, discussions and arguments. No clear direction can be set or decision made. Division, rebellion, complaining and confusion will be the result.

Growth in numbers will be prevented because authority will not be respected, nor will it be possible to delegate authority.

If there is not submission to the Holy Spirit, the group degenerates into humanism, theological debate and religious politics. Notice here that no "vote" was taken. This is not a committee, but a group of saints seeking the will of God. I used to describe our method at the Tikkun leadership meetings as "pray and talk pray and talk" until we come to unity. All human viewpoints are imperfect. It is not "our will" we seek, but "His will" (**Matthew 26:39**). All of us are "wrong." We need the help of a "third" party. It is possible to hear the voice of the Holy Spirit if we humble ourselves and pray.

There is debate whether leadership structure in the New Covenant is "royal" (hierarchical authority with a single head leader) or "fraternal" (a group of equals with no vertical authority). On the one hand, since authority comes "downward" from heaven and is delegated through Yeshua, there has to be clear vertical authority.

On the other hand, since every believer has the right to receive the Holy Spirit, we have to hear from one another as brothers and sisters. The answer is obviously a blend and balance of the two positions. (See *Covenant Relationships*, chapter 29, on "Headship with Plurality.")

In 2012, our congregation in Jerusalem had to change meeting location and time. There seemed to be no good solution. Whatever we were to decide, some members would be happy, and others not. We saw that people's differences of opinion were heating up. We called for prayer and fasting. Then we held an open congregational meeting. The elders explained that this meeting was not to make a decision but to listen to one another. One sister asked if we would take a vote. I explained the principles of New Covenant congregational decision making and that voting is not our method but to seek God's will.

After that the leadership met again and prayed and discussed the issue. Finally, we had a sense of direction. The weight of the final decision fell primarily to Eddie Santoro and myself as the elders. While some were still hurt and offended, all knew that we had sought God's will, that the discernments of all were considered, and that finally the leadership made a clear decision.

In the end, despite the difficulties, the congregation was blessed and began to grow both spiritually and numerically. Sometimes there is no perfect answer. The integrity has to do with the process of the decision making, not necessarily the final outcome.

In delegating and decision-making, we are always in two positions, "in" authority and "under" authority. We need to know how to handle both positions – *up-line* and *down-line* - how to submit under someone else's authority and how to treat those under our authority (**Luke 7:8**).

When we are in a position under authority, we should lean as far as possible toward the "royal" model, giving the leader the benefit of the doubt, affirming his authority and demonstrating submission. When we are in a position of leadership, we should lean as far as possible toward the "fraternal" model, listening to those serving under our authority, treating them as brothers and sisters, respecting their opinion.

Human nature tends to do just the *opposite*. We clamor for a more fraternal approach in any group where we are under authority. Then when we are in leadership, we expect those around us to respect and submit to our authority. Most people make both mistakes in both directions. If we fight against that selfish tendency, we come closer to the godly balance.

Once I had the opportunity to work on a conference in Jerusalem with **Jack Hayford**, the well-respected, senior leader of the Four-Square denomination. I was surprised how deferring and polite he was to everyone around him. He had clear authority to make the decisions, but he treated all the others as if they were the leaders and he was serving them. In his humility and sensitivity, his leadership stood out even more. I thought he was being too polite and over-sensitive. However, I realized that his sensitivity and deference had been born out of years of real experience working with leaders, who unfortunately can be so easily offended and insulted.

There are two strikingly different styles of dialogue in the epistles of Titus and Philemon. In Titus, Paul exercises executive authority at the highest level.

Titus 1:5

I left you in Crete that you should set in order the things that are lacking, and appoint elders in every city as I commanded you.

Here Paul is acting like an arch-bishop with total hierarchal authority. There is no discussion. Paul states, "I command you." Paul acts in authority with Titus whom he has set over the churches to appoint their leadership. There could be no clearer example of direct vertical authority than this.

This communication says something about Titus. Paul felt comfortable with Titus. He knew Titus received his authority. Paul did not have to worry about Titus being offended or insulted. Titus had apparently gone out of his way over the years to demonstrate his soldier-like submission to Paul. This freed Paul to act with speed and decisiveness. Together they were able to multiply churches in an entire nation.

This style is in stark contrast to Philemon. Paul writes to Philemon with a request to receive back his former slave Onesimus as a brother in the Lord. [Although this seems to be a simple request, it had social, economic and even historic implications.] Paul dedicates the majority of the letter to addressing Philemon personably, in a deferring manner, going out of his way not to offend him. This says something about the complexity of the subject and of Paul's relationship to Philemon; there is not the same directness as in the Titus letter. Paul had to "cushion" his request.

In 2014, Youval Yanay became the general director of Revive Israel ministries. He and I spoke with our team about the Titus-Philemon dynamic. When we are under authority, we want to treat the leader as Titus did to Paul. When we are in authority, we want to treat others as Paul did to Philemon. We act like Titus to Paul in the upward direction; and like Paul to Philemon in the downward direction. Over time, everyone will build trust and confidence to let authority flow more efficiently and effectively. Then we can move away from Philemon-like oversensitivity toward Titus-like confidence.

QUESTIONS FOR REFLECTION:

What three elements did the first century disciples use in resolving conflict in Acts 15?

What is the difference between "royal" and "fraternal" authority structures?

What is the best way for leadership to function in a New Covenant leadership system? Why do you think so?

CHAPTER 19
CONGREGATIONAL DISCIPLINE

Yeshua is the head of God's authority in heaven and on earth. As believers in Yeshua, we become a spiritual link between that heavenly and earthly authority. The ***ecclesia-kehilah*** (church) is therefore a body of spiritual authority. The first act that Yeshua did in starting the ecclesia was to transfer authority to it that connects heaven and earth. This authority is called "keys" and "binding and loosing."

Matthew 16:18-19

...on this rock I will build my church

...I give you the keys of the kingdom of heaven; whatever you bind on earth will be bound in heaven and whatever you loose on earth will be loosed in heaven.

Yeshua repeats the term "binding and loosing" in Matthew 18. The Matthew 16 passage describes the transfer of spiritual authority; Matthew 18 describes the operation of that authority within the ecclesia.

Matthew 18:15-18

If your brother sins against you, go and tell him his fault between you and him alone. If he hears you, you have gained your brother. If he will not hear, take with you one or two more, that by the mouth of two or three witnesses, every word may be established. If he refuses to hear them, tell it to the church. If he refuses even to hear the church, let him be to you like a heathen and a tax collector. Whatever you bind on earth will be bound in heaven, and whatever you loose on earth will be loosed in heaven.

This passage in Matthew 18 is foundational to covenantal relationships, to church government, and to any kind of community authority. Some question whether Matthew 18 authority is spiritual or religious. In context it is addressing moral and relational issues. [Here we will deal with it only briefly as it is explained in depth in *Covenant Relationships*.]

In Matthew 16, Yeshua is passing on to His disciples the key of authority promised to David in **Isaiah 9:6** and **22:22.** In fact He expands the singular "key" given to David to the multiple "keys" given to Peter (**Matthew 16:19**). [Perhaps this refers to the expansion of the kingdom by the apostles in the first century from one key for Israel to many keys for the rest of the nations.]

The key of David is then preserved spiritually through the church of Philadelphia (**Revelation 3:7-8, 11**). [The fact that a Davidic key is preserved represents a veiled promise for a future restoration of Jerusalem-centered, kingdom and apostolic authority in the end times.]

Authority in Yeshua's kingdom operates through covenant and personal relationships. There is authority in the home through the covenant of marriage; in business through contract; in government by citizenship; in the local congregation by membership.

Covenant is a commitment to long-term relationships. The local congregation is not supposed to be a theater where one buys a ticket (the tithe), sits in the audience, enjoys the show, and goes home. It is supposed to be an extended spiritual "second" family.

In this congregational family, the first rule is simple: no gossip. We make a commitment not to speak negatively about someone behind his back. If there is a problem, you talk to the person alone. Imagine how wonderful it would be to be part of a community where at least there was this one rule. The first covenant "commandment": Do not talk negatively about anyone behind his back.

This passage also describes a process of congregational discipline. The process is personal and patient, compassionate and caring. The emphasis is on moral and interpersonal problems, not so much ritual or theological problems. The process does involve discipline. To have discipline, there must be authority. The ecclesia not only has heavenly authority, the local congregation has authority for moral discipline within its membership.

There is no physical punishment in the church. That realm belongs to the government when a crime has been committed. Spiritual authority in the sphere of the congregation is limited first to moral rebuke, and then finally to remove the person's privilege to be a member. By the time the conflict reaches this stage, the person sinning usually does not want to be in the congregation anyway.

Part of the purpose of removing the person from congregational membership is to create social pressure to influence him to change for the good. Another purpose is to prevent negative influence from affecting others (**I Corinthians 15:33**).

However, there is also spiritual protection in the congregation under the authority of the elders. The punishment, therefore, is to remove this protection. At that point the person is exposed to additional spiritual attack. The hope is that the awareness of the damage caused by the person's own sin would cause him to repent; in which case he would be received back into the congregational family and covering.

The members of the congregation must recognize the authority of the elders to rebuke sin, remove someone from membership, and restore to membership. The authority works both ways. In the church at Corinth, a member committed adultery and incest – and remained unrepentant. Paul demanded that he be removed from membership, thus, exposing him to attack from the devil in the hope of restoring him in the future.

I Corinthians 5:5

Deliver such a one to Satan for the destruction of the flesh, so that his spirit might be saved in the day of the Lord.

The elders in the congregation were apparently reluctant to enforce discipline, so Paul as the apostle had to step in to exercise authority. In this case the discipline was successful, and the man repented. Here the elders missed the opportunity to restore the man, and so Paul had to step in again.

II Corinthians 2:6-7, 11

The punishment inflicted by the majority was sufficient for such a man. On the contrary, you ought to forgive and comfort him... lest Satan should take advantage of us; for we are not ignorant of his devices.

In I Corinthians Paul exercises congregational discipline to remove the man; in II Corinthians to receive him back. In I Corinthians Paul removes the man's protection; in II Corinthians restores it. The devil had a two-sided attack:

1. Temptation toward sin

2. Condemnation about sin

In I Corinthians, Paul dealt with the demonic influence of temptation to sin, and in II Corinthians with the demonic influence of "accusation of the saints" (**Revelation 12:10**).

The elders have to protect the flock from both attacks. They rebuke sin when it is committed and forgive sin when it is repented of. Thus they "bind" and "loose." They judge and pardon.

This congregational discipline is a type of "Pre-Judgment Day", judgment in order that we will not have to be judged on Judgment Day itself. Can you imagine this man coming before the throne of God? Satan comes to accuse him. God turns to Paul to ask his opinion. Paul responds, "This man is no longer guilty. The elders disciplined him because of the sin and then in the name of Yeshua forgave him of his sins after he repented." God says, "That's fine. What you bound on earth will be bound here in heaven. This higher court receives the decision of the lower court. Case closed."

Members of the congregation need to recognize the moral and spiritual authority of the elders to make judgment on moral and spiritual issues if congregational discipline is to be effective. The elders have authority within the local congregation. If the matter becomes inter-congregational or if the elders need support, the case transfers over to the elders and apostles together (**Acts 15:2, 4, 6, 22**).

I Corinthians 6:2-3

Do you not know that the saints will judge the world? And if the world will be judged by you, are you unworthy to judge the smallest of matters? Do you not know that we will judge angels? How much more things that pertain to this life?

The sphere of judicial authority in the congregation is with the elders. The sphere in the greater Body is with the apostles. The congregational sphere of justice is for members only on moral issues. The sphere of justice outside the congregation for criminal matters is in the hands of the civil courts. Eternal judgment we leave to God.

It is important that the local elders, city-wide elders and even national leaders have a mechanism for judicial appeal on moral issues to ensure the safety of the members in congregations across the body.

To take an issue of congregational discipline before the civil courts would be a violation of spheres of judicial authority and an embarrassment to the congregation.

I Corinthians 6:5-7

I say this to your shame. Brother goes to court against brother, and that before unbelievers! It is already an utter failure.

The system of justice with the ecclesia is one of holiness and grace. We deal with higher moral standards than a civil court would care about. Yet we are also committed to the hope of forgiveness not condemnation. The goal of congregational discipline is to **"win your brother"** back in love (**Matthew 18:15**). We guard against both guilt-manipulation and sin (**John 8:11; II Corinthians 2:11**). It is the function of Satan to accuse and condemn (**Revelation 12:10**). Yeshua is the "advocate" (**I John 2:1**). We are judges with Him on the side of "advocacy."

Let us recognize congregational authority with the local elders, while requiring the elders to walk in integrity and faithfulness themselves. Let us strive for the balance of holiness and grace. Let us build covenant communities where we do not speak evil of one another, where moral standards are maintained, and where we are committed to life-long relationships.

QUESTIONS FOR REFLECTION:

What is the primary purpose of the ecclesia-kehila (church)?

How does spiritual authority operate within a local congregation?

What two attacks do elders serve to protect congregants from?

What is the goal of congregational discipline according to Matthew 18?

PART THREE:
KINGDOM AUTHORITY

CHAPTER 20
APOSTOLIC TEAM MINISTRY

In our generation God is restoring the functions of apostles and prophets within the Body of Messiah. As deacons have responsibility for areas of service within the congregation and elders the authority to govern the local congregation, apostles represent a third level of leadership dealing with the wider body. The apostles and their ministry teams seek to train new leaders, build and unite the body of Messiah, advance the kingdom of God, and oversee the prophets, evangelists, pastors and teachers.

This is what we mean when we say "apostolic team ministry."

Ephesians 4:11-13

He himself gave some to be apostles, some to be prophets, some to be evangelists, and some pastors and teachers for the equipping of the saints for the work of the ministry, for the edifying of the body of Messiah, until we all come to the unity of the faith...

There are listed here five different kinds of ministry leaders. They are referred to as the "five-fold" ministry or "gift" ministry offices. Much has been written about their roles in recent years, so here we will touch on the subject only briefly as it pertains to spheres of authority. The five types of ministers are supposed to work together in cooperation. Part of the apostle's function is to coordinate that teamwork.

The pastor acts as the coordinator/overseer of the elders, and the apostle acts as the coordinator/overseer of the five-fold ministers. The apostle acts as the pastor of the prophets, evangelists, pastors and teachers. The pastor is the primary leader of the local congregation, but he is submitted to the authority of the apostle. The apostle lays vision and foundations of the local congregation (**I Corinthians 3:10**) and sets in order and oversees its structure (**Titus 1:5**).

This list of ministry gifts in **Ephesians 4** represents both function and office. It is possible to function in one of the gifts listed but on a lower authority level. Any person in the congregation can prophesy, teach or evangelize. Those functions can be done on a congregant's level, an elder level or on a five-fold office level. A person must operate on an elder level before he can operate in a five-fold office. Elders are assistants to the pastor who is the leader of the elders. An apostle must serve as an elder and pastor before operating in the office of apostle.

In order for the body of Messiah to grow, there must be cooperation between leaders. For there to be cooperation, there must be recognition of different types of gifts and callings. Presently, in many parts of the church, without understanding five-fold ministry, everyone called to leadership will try to be a pastor. This can be counter-productive, even destructive, as it causes the pastor to strive to function essentially in all five offices by himself. The vast majority of us are not fit, called or gifted for such broad service. Also, he will tend to see himself in competition with other pastors. He works himself into a lonely corner in the congregation. Burn-out is on the way before he even gets started.

The main point here is that we need to build on a team-work model of leadership and not a one-man show. **Ephesians 4** gives us a model for different types of leaders working together in cooperation.

If there is no coordinator/overseer for the different types of ministers then an inherent conflict of interest will arise. The prophet thinks about God more than about the people; the evangelist thinks about the unsaved, while the pastor thinks about the flock – and the teacher about Bible study! The job of the apostle is to help them work together like the players on a basketball team. Everyone should know what position to play and how to help one another in order to win the game.

Our team at Revive Israel studied models of apostolic/prophetic teams we saw in the Scriptures.

- There were predecessors in the Israelite prophets (like Elijah, Elisha, Samuel and others), who had a school of younger prophets around them (**I Samuel 10:5, II Kings 2:15**).

- Yeshua and the twelve is the foundational model. They functioned primarily as a traveling band of healing evangelists (**Luke 9:1-2**). (Later they became the leadership of the first congregation in **Acts 242-43**.)

- Peter likely had a similar team of healing evangelists around him, including John Mark.

- John likely had a group of devotionally-oriented, prophetically-gifted people around him.

- The congregation at Antioch became a base for sending out multiple types of ministries (**Acts 13:1-3**).

- Paul had a traveling team with a multi-level staff, including assistant apostles, pastors, a doctor, a scribe who penned his letters, a treasurer who kept track of the offerings, and administrative assistants who brought his books and clothes.

- Paul at one point changed style to stay two years in Ephesus in order to run a discipleship training school (**Acts 19**).

- James served as bishop of Jerusalem over the council of churches (**Acts 15:13-20**).

- The five-fold ministry listed in **Ephesians 4:11-13** shows a teamwork of leaders at the highest level of cooperation, maturity and effectiveness for the kingdom of God.

There are different types of teaching styles in the body. Teachers present principles of Scripture systematically. Pastors encourage and edify the flock. Evangelists create revival dynamism and power in the assembly. Prophets bring conviction of heart and revelation of the Spirit. The apostle has a different approach, focusing on the overall kingdom of God, foundations of the Church, the restoration of Israel, the outpouring of the Holy Spirit, and the completing of the great commission.

The teaching of the Apostles was central to the first-century community.

Acts 2:42

They continued steadfastly in the apostles' teaching...

The teaching of apostles today has less importance than in the first century, because we have the complete Bible which contains authoritative Apostolic teaching (**II Timothy 3:16**), and the pastors and teachers can readily teach from the Bible in the congregations. In addition, apostles (small "a") today are not "The Apostles" (capital "A") of the Lamb. Yet, Bible teaching from the perspective of apostles within the body today is still greatly needed.

They provide vision and foundation, anointing and authority, in a way which the other ministers do not. There is apostolic breakthrough for miracles, finances, revival, multiplication, and kingdom strategy. (See supplement 16 on "Apostolic Miracle Breakthroughs.") We cannot have action like the Acts of the Apostles, if we do not receive the ministry of apostles today.

Some do not believe that there are apostles other than the original Twelve. The story of Barnabas proves that there are other apostles (**Acts 14:14**) and even describes the stages of development in the process of his becoming an apostle. (See supplement 17 on "Three Stages of Barnabas.")

As the congregation is the sphere of authority of the pastor, an apostle has a group of congregations and ministries in his sphere. As pastors respect one another's churches, so must the spheres of the apostles' ministries be clarified and respected.

Paul and Barnabas became apostles at the same time. This caused tension between them. Paul could have submitted to Barnabas; or, Barnabas could have submitted to Paul; they chose instead to go their own directions, which separated and clarified their spheres of authority (**Acts 15:36-41**).

One of Paul's most difficult spiritual battles was defending his apostolic authority. We often quote **II Corinthians 10:3-5** about spiritual warfare. Notice that the context of this passage is Paul's defense of his authority – a large section of Scriptures extending from **II Corinthians 9** all the way through chapter **13.** Understanding Paul's spiritual battles as a defense of his apostolic authority is profound and enlightening.

The tension between Paul and James is seen in **Acts 15** and **Acts 21**, yet it comes to a full reconciliation in both cases. The tension between Paul and Peter is apparent in **Galatians 1**, yet it also comes to total reconciliation as expressed by Peter's admiration of Paul in **II Peter 3:15-16**. Because of jealousy and competition, Paul tried to serve in areas where others were not working (**Romans 15:20; II Corinthians 10:15**).

The context for our key verses concerning spheres of spiritual authority is connected to Paul's defense of apostolic ministry against the complaints of others.

II Corinthians 10:8, 13-16

If I should boast about our authority, which the Lord gave us for edification and not for destruction, I shall not be ashamed. We will not boast beyond measure, but within the limits of the sphere which God appointed us – a sphere which especially includes you. For we are not over extending ourselves (as though our authority did not extend to you), for it was to you that we came with the gospel... not boasting of things beyond measure, in other men's labors, but... greatly enlarged by you in our sphere ...not to boast in another man's sphere of accomplishment.

Since an apostle's function is for the wider body, rather than a particular congregation, part of the apostle's concern is for unity. Unity is mentioned twice in **Ephesians 4**. The first time refers to the work of the Holy Spirit: **"endeavoring to keep the unity of the Spirit"** – **verse 3**, which speaks of one faith, one hope and one Lord. The second refers to the work of apostles: **"edifying the body of Messiah until we all come to the unity of faith"** – **verse 12-13.** To reach the goal of maturity and unity in love, we need both the intervention of the Holy Spirit and the ministry of apostolic teams.

QUESTIONS FOR REFLECTION:

What are the five ministry gifts described in Ephesians 4?

Which of the five ministry gifts coordinates the cooperation of the five-fold ministry team?

What was one of Paul's most difficult spiritual battles?

What is a primary purpose of apostolic leadership?

CHAPTER 21
SEATED WITH HIM

Spiritual authority is an expression of the ascension of Yeshua. The ascension of Yeshua is mentioned three times in Ephesians. Chapter 1 describes Yeshua's ascent back into heaven above all powers and principalities (verses 20-21). Chapter 2 describes how we are seated together with Him in that place above the principalities (verse 6). Chapter 4 explains that through the ascension, Yeshua established the offices of the five-fold ministry (verses 8-13). The apostolic team could also be called, "Ascension Offices."

In **Ephesians 1:16-17** Paul prays that we would have a revelation of how the ascension of Yeshua affects us as believers. We began discussing this in the chapter "Regaining our Spiritual Authority." The power of God works in us according to Yeshua's crucifixion, His resurrection and His ascension. By the crucifixion we have forgiveness of sins, by the resurrection we have eternal life, and by the ascension we have spiritual authority. What does this mean?

During the Old Covenant period, Yeshua visited the earth as the Angel of YHVH. He appeared to Abraham as the "judge of all the earth" (**Genesis 18:25**) before the destruction of Sodom. He appeared to Moses as deliverer at the crossing of the Red Sea (**Exodus 14:19**) and as the Law-giver on Mount Sinai (**Exodus 24:10-12**). He appeared as the commander of the armies of heaven to Joshua (**Joshua 5:13-14**), as the glorified King to Isaiah (**Isaiah 6:1**), as the God-man over the Cherubim to Ezekiel (**Ezekiel 1:26**), and the man of fire to Daniel (**Daniel 10:4-6**). (This is explained in detail in our book, "*Who Ate Lunch with Abraham?*")

When Yeshua came during the Old Covenant, He only visited temporarily. In the New Covenant He was born into the earth permanently. In the Old Covenant He came in the appearance of a man, but in the New Covenant He actually became a man. In the Old Covenant He rescued us as God helping mankind. In the New Covenant He saved us as Man leading mankind. He is the same person, but His status has changed.

Yeshua could not have been crucified until after He was born into this earth, because He had to bear our punishment as a man. Yeshua could not have been resurrected until He had died as a man. Because He was a man, He could pass on to us what He acquired by the crucifixion and the resurrection.

Here is the next stage of revelation: the same holds true for the ascension. Yeshua was seated in heaven with all authority long before His birth on earth. But He was not fully human when He sat there. He gave up that position to be born into the earth as a man (**Philippians 2:5-9**). When He was raised from the dead, He then had authority in heaven and earth as the God-Man (**Matthew 28:18**), sort of a new species: not just human being but a resurrected human being.

When Yeshua returned to heaven, He returned to the same position He already had before being born into this earth. However, this time He returned to that place as a man. He was "as if" a man before that (**Ezekiel 1:26**), but now He is truly a man. He is both God and man. He sits in heaven at the highest place of authority as a man who was born, crucified and resurrected.

There is a God-Man seated in heaven above all powers and principalities. He is not only a resurrected human being but a resurrected-ascended human being. By His ascension, He opens up to us the possibility of sharing that same position of divine authority above all things in creation. Let's read the passage again:

Ephesians 1:19 -22

... according to the working of his mighty power, which he worked in Messiah when he raised him from the dead and seated him at his right hand in heavenly places, far above all principality and power, might and dominion..., not only in this age but also in that which is to come. And he put all things under his feet, and gave him to be head over all things to the church.

If Yeshua already had all authority, why did He go through all this? – In order to share it with us! How could He transfer authority to us if He himself was not a man? – He couldn't. Therefore, He became a man. As He transferred salvation to us as a man through the cross and the resurrection, so He transferred authority to us through the ascension.

There is a born-again man sitting on the throne at the highest place in heaven. If He is there, we can join Him. In the Old Covenant He was there, but we could not be there with Him. Since He is now a man, we can join Him. Born-again humans now have access to the throne in a way that was never possible before. If it is possible for Him to be there, it is possible for us to be there.

Ephesians 2:6

Raised us up together, and made us sit together in the heavenly places in Messiah Yeshua.

If He is there, we are there – by outrageous, undeserved, extravagant grace! Yeshua made all that effort to re-establish authority in heaven and earth from the position as a born-again man. So there He is, in heaven, above all power and principality. What is He going to do about it? Just sit there? No, He wants to share it with us.

First, He gives us access by the Holy Spirit in prayer and faith to be seated with Him on that throne (**Ephesians 2:6**). Then He transfers the authority in heaven above all kingdoms to His body: the ecclesia-kehilah-church.

Ephesians 1:22-23

... put all things under his feet, and gave him to be head over all things to the church, which is his body, the fullness of him who fills all in all.

What would you do if you had all authority to yourself? Yeshua doesn't want to rule the universe by Himself. He wants to share it with us. He wants to rule **through us.** He will rule over us, and we will rule the universe under His authority. He is the head; we are the body; all things are under our "feet."

It wouldn't be logical, even for Yeshua, to try to rule the universe alone. In any kind of kingdom or society, authority must be delegated. There must be a representative body who will govern the people. Yeshua rules the ecclesia; the ecclesia rules the world under His headship. Yeshua is King Messiah; the church is His Bride-Queen, co-reigning with Him.

Yeshua is in heaven above all powers and principalities (**Ephesians 1:21**). We are seated there with Him (**Ephesians 2:6**). He delegates His authority to the ecclesia (**Ephesians 1:22**). How does He delegate authority to rule the world from heaven through the ecclesia? – by creating a system of delegated authority within the ecclesia. That includes deacons, elders, pastors and also prophets and apostles.

Ephesians 4:8-11

When he ascended on high, he led captivity captive and gave gifts to men...

He who descended is also the one who ascended far above all the heavens, that he might fill all things, and he himself gave some to be apostles, some prophets...

At the ascension Yeshua "gave gifts." He created positions of spiritual authority. Yeshua ascended and regained kingdom authority. He delegated that authority to the ecclesia by creating "gifts offices" within the ecclesia. He "gave" them to us. We can call them "ascension gifts" or "ascension offices." These gifts are not just positions of authority, but spiritually "gifted" people to fill those positions.

The New Covenant five-fold gifts are offices of authority that Yeshua created when He ascended to heaven. He transfers spiritual authority to people of His favor here on earth. Positions of authority today within the ecclesia, family, government or workplace are preparatory positions in order to govern in the world to come. In any coalition government, there are levels of delegated authority under the Prime Minister. Likewise, there are levels of spiritual authority within the body of King Messiah.

By the ascension, Yeshua regained all authority (**Ephesians 1:21**). He transfers the authority to the ecclesia, His body (**Ephesians 1:22**). His authority is granted equally and spiritually to **all** believers, since we can all be "seated with Him" in heaven (**Ephesians 2:6**). It is also delegated hierarchically through various positions of authority within the body, including the five-fold ministries (**Ephesians 4:11**).

[**Note 1:** Spiritual authority in the ecclesia today is a transition from the Old Covenant in the past to the millennial kingdom in the future. New Covenant five-fold ministry is a continuation of the spiritual authority given to the Old Covenant prophets, who were **"set over the nations and over the kingdoms"** - **Jeremiah 1:10**. What we are talking about here is a continuation, development and improvement of what Jeremiah and the other prophets already had.]

[**Note 2:** Spiritual authority is transferred to all believers inside the name "Yeshua." A name identifies who a person is and also his function and position of authority. Yeshua has the **"name above all names"** – **Mark 16:17, Acts 4:7, 12, Ephesians 1:21, Philippians 2:9**. When we have His name, we have the authority that goes with it.]

[**Note 3:** Yeshua's authority is not only in heaven (angels) and on earth (men), but also under the earth (demons). For this reason, He descended under the earth between the cross and the resurrection and destroyed the forces of hell and Satan – **Mathew 12:40, Acts 2:31, Romans 10:7, Ephesians 4:9, I Peter 3:19, 4:6, Revelation 1:18**. He passes on to us those same three levels of authority – "in heaven, on earth and under the earth" - **Philippians 2:10.**]

All this is to say the following: there is great reason and motivation for us to get over all the attitude problems we have about authority; because in the long run, when we submit to

God's authority, He desires to transfer it to us and share it with us. Let's overcome our attitude problems about authority and realize how much God is trying to bless us! Let's see the glorious plan and destiny that God has had for us from the beginning.

QUESTIONS FOR REFLECTION:

By what three ways does the power of God work in us?

What are the benefits of these three ways?

What is the difference between the status of the Son in the Old Covenant and the New Covenant?

How does Yeshua delegate the authority of His ascension back to the Body on earth?

What is the great reason and motivation for us to work out our issues with authority?

CHAPTER 22
MESSIANIC APOSTOLIC MINISTRY

In the early 1980's some of us in the Messianic Jewish movement were exposed to the restoration of apostles and prophets in the Body of Messiah. For those of us in the Washington, D.C. and Baltimore area in the United States, we were blessed to participate in local "New Testament" apostolic networks. The question arose as to whether we should continue as Messianic guests or join fully as members in their network.

In 1984 a few of us took some time out to pray and fast about the issue. Dan Juster (as leader of our group and pastor at Beth Messiah congregation), Eitan Shishkoff, Michael Rudolph, Moshe Morrison and I were involved. We sensed from the Lord that we were to stay in relationship with the prophetic and apostolic networks, yet we were to start our own five-fold ministry team as Messianic believers.

We didn't understand all the implications, but the Lord was with us. The team started as "BMAM" – Beth Messiah Apostolic Ministries. A few years later, we took on the name "Tikkun" from the rabbinic concept of "world restoration." Apostolic ministry, world restoration, and Messianic Judaism seemed to fit together perfectly. (See Supplement 18, on "Restoration of All Things.")

Dan was released from being pastor at Beth Messiah as our first apostle with Eitan becoming the pastor. I was sent to plant a new congregation, called El Shaddai Congregation. Paul Wilbur was released into his own worship-evangelistic ministry with Marc Chopinsky and Renee Block, called Israel's Hope. Moshe Morrison became the pastor at Rosh Pina in Baltimore and Michael Rudolph at Ahavat Yeshua in Washington, D.C.

In 1985 Michael Brown joined our team. He and I served as "prophets" on the team (with an embarrassing amount of over-zealousness and immaturity on our parts!). Other congregations joined us. The Bible college grew under Dr. Brown's direction. Israel's Hope albums became number one best sellers. Many Jewish people came to faith in Yeshua, and new congregations were planted. Later we were joined by Gateways Beyond ministries with David Rudolph and Caleb Company with Don Finto.

We had a sense that in the future, there would be three networks: one in the US with Dan (Tikkun), one in Haifa-northern Israel with Eitan (Ohalei Rachamim) and one in Jerusalem-Tel Aviv corridor with me (Revive Israel). More recently Dan and Patty have made Aliya to join us here in Israel.

Approximately 10 years before it happened I had a clear sense that I would be moving to Israel in 1992. I rarely ever receive prophetic discernments with dates, so this was unusual. Later Eitan discerned that he was to move to Israel in the same year.

[Note: I am only describing what happened in our team. Of course God also raised up other Messianic apostolic ministry teams in various locations around the world, both inside and outside of Israel, and in the former Soviet Union. We consider the ministry networks out of Philadelphia connected to the Chernoff family to have an apostolic calling, as well Jews for Jesus, Chosen People, and many others.]

Jonathan Bernis started his apostolic-evangelistic ministry in the Ukraine in 1992 as well. Dan seemed impressed that the date had significance, although I had never thought about it. We had an inner assurance to make Aliyah in 1992. We did so, along with several other Messianic leaders as well.

[**Note:** Later it occurred to us that the most significant date in Jewish history between the destruction of the Second Temple and the birth of the State of Israel was the expulsion of the Jews from Spain (1492). That year Columbus sailed for America after the Treaty of Granada between the Catholic and Muslim empires was signed. By a strange "God-coincidence," 1992 corresponded to the 500 year anniversary of those events.]

To describe the development of the body of Messiah and apostolic ministry in Israel or growth of Messianic congregations around the world would require another book altogether. At the time of this writing, there are over 100 congregations or fellowships in Israel, most of them small (and upwards of 1000 groups worldwide). Despite multi-faceted and indescribable spiritual attacks, the body continues to grow little by little every year.

The Messianic Jewish remnant in Israel today is a partial restoration of the first-century community of disciples. The emergence of apostolic-prophetic ministry teams within that remnant is an initial restoration of the ministries of those original apostles and prophets. (Of course their great glory and our manifest weakness make even the comparison quite embarrassing. However, the spiritual parallel is significant nonetheless.)

[**Note:** Many international ministries come to Israel today in a variety of capacities and are more than welcome. In this chapter, however, we are speaking of the local community of faith, led primarily by Israeli believers and established within the language, culture, economy, history and world view of our people. See Supplement 19, "Integrity of Indigenous Ministry in Israel."]

There is a modern Hebrew expression, "To see the one born," meaning that when something small is started, you can discern what it will be when it grows. Although it is still in its "baby" stages, we believe that the Messianic remnant in Israel will have a certain role to play in the fulfillment of end times' prophecy. (See Supplement 20, "The Fig Tree and the Second Coming.")

In **Acts 1** the disciples received the great commission and the promise of the outpouring of the Holy Spirit. In **Acts 2** on Pentecost (Shavuot) morning, they were filled with the power of the Holy Spirit in tongues of fire. Between the promise and the outpouring, the disciples gave themselves to fervent, united prayer.

Acts 1:14

These all continued with one accord in prayer and supplication.

United prayer leads to revival. Yet there was another element between the prayer and the outpouring: the appointment of the 12th apostle. The second half of **Acts 1** deals with Judas' replacement. At first glance, that appointment doesn't seem significant. After all there were still the other 11 apostles. However, the restoration of the 12th apostle was important to them in order to preserve the covenant pattern of the 12 tribes of Israel. It had symbolic significance like the 12 stones of Elijah's altar (**I Kings 18:31**) and the 12 stones of Joshua's memorial (**Joshua 4:2-3**).

The re-appointment of the 12th apostle seems to me somewhat symbolic of the restoration of an apostolic-prophetic Messianic remnant in Israel today. At the same time, God is raising up a world-wide network of united prayer (with much thanks to our dear friends at the *International House of Prayer,* led by Mike Bickle, and leaders of other prayer movements worldwide).

The parallel emergence of a united international prayer network and a Messianic remnant in Israel is a sign that we are moving toward a historic end times' revival. We believe that a greater revival than what is recorded in **Acts 2** will take place. God's Spirit will be poured out on all nations and upon a local revival here in Israel. (See Supplement 21, "Second Pentecost.")

The promise of world revival as recorded in **Acts 2:17- "In the last days I will pour out my Spirit on all flesh"** is a quote from the prophet Joel. In context Joel is speaking of a revival which is connected to the Messianic remnant in Israel during the end times. The Holy Spirit will be poured out on all flesh…

Joel 2:32 – 3:1

… because there will be a remnant in Mount Zion and in Jerusalem … among the survivors whom YHVH has called … for I will restore the captivity of Judah and Jerusalem.

The Hebrew text of Joel seems to be a prophetic hint that in the generation of those who survived the Holocaust, God will restore the nation of Israel and the city of Jerusalem. Then God will call unto salvation a remnant of faith among the Jews in Israel. When this remnant is in place, the conditions will be set for the end times' prophecies to come to pass. These include both the negative prophecies of world disasters and the positive prophecies of world revival.

In **Acts 15** the historic apostolic council took place to discuss the development of the Gentile churches. They made a gracious, strategic decision to encourage the churches internationally to grow without having to keep Jewish cultural traditions. These instructions were sent around the world. The result was that the churches began to grow and multiply.

Acts 16:4-5

They went through the cities and delivered to them the decrees to keep which were determined by the apostles and elders in Jerusalem. So the churches were strengthened in the faith, and increased in number daily.

The churches in cities around the world grew in numbers *daily* after receiving instructions from the apostles in Jerusalem. Gentile churches do not need to submit to Messianic leaders from Israel today. However, as we move more into the end times, there will be vital, strategic impartation for the international church coming out of the body in Israel. The right alignment with love and humility between the Messianic remnant and the international Church could release a great breakthrough.

I believe that the alignment of the international Church with the Messianic remnant in Israel re-establishes a covenant pattern of kingdom authority that will help prepare both Israel and the Church for the Second Coming of Yeshua and the establishment of His kingdom on earth.

Unfortunately, many of us in the Messianic movement have spread teachings that were unbalanced and unedifying. We ask forgiveness for our errors, and we hope that God will heal and bring the blessing He has promised.

One blessing that should come out of the relationship between the Messianic remnant and the international Church is unity. As there is unity in the spirit through prayer as described in **John 17**, so is there unity through being grafted into the same historic root as described in **Romans 11**. We are united by being connected in spirit to the grape vine (**John 15**) and in covenant to the olive tree (**Romans 11**).

We pray that the Messianic remnant will be a source of unity, blessing and glory to the greater body of Messiah on one side and to the nation of Israel on the other side. (See Supplement 22, on "John 17 and Romans 11 Unity.") The unity between the international Church and the remnant of Israel is also described a "one new man" in Ephesians, chapters 2 and 3.

Isaiah 60:1-3

Arise, shine; for your light has come! And the glory of YHVH has risen upon you. For behold, the darkness shall cover the earth, and deep darkness the people; but YHVH will arise over you, and His glory will be seen upon you. The Gentiles will come to your light and kings to the brightness of your rising.

In the end times, certainly great evil will cover the whole world. Yet at the same time, God's glorious destiny for Israel and the Church will emerge.

QUESTIONS FOR REFLECTION:

To what degree is Messianic Judaism in Israel a restoration of the original apostolic community?

Why was it important for there to be 12 apostles in the first century?

What is one blessing that should come of the relationship between the Messianic Remnant and the International Church?

CHAPTER 23
UNITING THE KINGDOM

To write this book my wife and I rented a small room on the banks of the Tiber in Rome, and before this chapter I walked up to Piazza San Pietro. I looked up to see the huge dome of the Vatican. It reminded me of the Capitol Dome in Washington, D.C. and of the Dome of the Rock on the Temple Mount in Jerusalem. It seems that domes are symbols of government, power and authority (perhaps representing the dome of the sky).

The Vatican dome is a symbol of Catholic power; the Capitol dome of United States power; the Dome of the Rock of Muslim power. They seem like an imitation of God's real kingdom authority.

Then I looked at the 13 large statues of Jewish men (Yeshua and the Apostles) on the roof of the Vatican, and the huge mural of Miriam, the young Jewish virgin mother of the Messiah, on the opposite wall.

(Unfortunately in Hebrew there is no difference between the word *statue* and the word *idol.* They are both *pesel;* a linguistic miscommunication which has caused negative reactions for centuries to Jews since they see statues as idols in Catholic cathedrals.)

There is something symbolic about Rome and Jerusalem. They represent two poles of authority. The book of Acts starts in Jerusalem and ends up in Rome. There is a spiritual movement that goes out from Jerusalem to Rome and is then to come back again.

God's kingdom authority has been divided and perverted throughout history, but God is in the process of purifying and uniting. The divisions are an attack of Satan (**Luke 11:17-22**). David and Solomon's kingdom was divided in two between Judah and Israel as a punishment from God (**I Kings 12**). The division between Judah and Israel provides a biblical pattern for understanding the split between Israel and the Church over the centuries.

The prophet Ezekiel had a vision of uniting the kingdom by placing two sticks in his hands, one for Judah and the sons of Israel, and one for Ephraim and the whole house of Israel (**Ezekiel 37:15-28**). I see this as a prophetic parable for the spiritual unity between Israel and the Church in the end times. (See Supplement 23, on "The Two Stick Prophecy.")

When Yeshua entered Jerusalem 2,000 years ago, He took a whip and cleansed the Temple by driving out the money changers and overthrowing the tables (**Matt. 21:12-13, John 2:13-17**). There is a paradox here. While we are called to recognize and respect God's delegated authority in all situations, the prophets of Israel devoted much of their energy to rebuking the kings and those in authority. The moral rebuke of those in authority was one of the major themes of the Hebrew prophets.

Jehu for example was anointed by the prophets to overthrow the government of Israel and to execute all the dynasty of Ahab and Jezebel (**II Kings chapters 9 & 10**). He was commanded by God, not to obey, submit or respect their authority, but to destroy them. This was an intervention of God to judge and punish those who had been in authority for their crimes.

Let us pray for a spirit of purity and repentance to cleanse both Judaism and Christianity of sin, error and religious hypocrisy before the coming of the Lord (**Malachi 3:1-5**), for Christians to be grafted in to their Israelite roots, and for Jews to come to faith in Yeshua the Messiah.

[For a discussion of the difference between institutional authority and charismatic leadership (and the equalizing effect of modern mass media and information systems on the younger generation), see Supplement 24, on "Millennial Authority" by Solomon Intrater.]

God cut a covenant with King David 1,000 years before the birth of Yeshua. In this covenant God promised to David and his seed the kingdom government authority on planet earth forever (**II Samuel 7:11-16**). Yeshua told His disciples that if they gave up all to follow Him, they would sit on 12 thrones judging the tribes of Israel (**Matt. 19:28**).

The number 12 for the tribes, the disciples, and the thrones indicates a continuation of the kingdom authority from the tribes of ancient Israel on to the apostles of Messiah.

In **Revelation 4:4** we find 24 elders on 24 thrones (the number 24 obviously being 2 times 12). This seems to be a doubling of the apostolic authority and may possibly represent the dual, cooperative authority of Israel and the Church.

When Yeshua saw that the Jewish religious leaders were about to reject Him and have Him crucified, He rebuked them strenuously as recorded in an entire chapter (**Matt. 23**). In the same chapter at the end of the same rebuke, Yeshua tells them that they will not see Him again until they say, "Blessed is He who comes in the name of the Lord" (**Baruch Haba Bashem Adonai,** ברוך הבא בשם ה') – **Matt. 23:39.** This statement set a pre-requisite for Yeshua's return.

There is a promise understood here that He will come back, and that they will indeed cry out, "Blessed is He who comes." The Church understands this statement as an *invitation*, similar to the cry *Marantha*, "Come Lord Jesus." And so it is. But it is more than an invitation; it is an inauguration. In the Hebrew, there is a word called *Hamlachah* - המלכה - from the root of "king" – *Melech* – מלך. The word *Hamlachah* means "to make someone king."

In some Jewish Chassidic literature, God will choose who is to be King Messiah, but the elders of Judah and Israel will do the *Hamlachah.* They will make the Messiah to be king. They will put him in office. This "king-making" of the Messiah by the affirmation and ordination of the elders of Jerusalem is seen as the continuation and application of God's covenant with David that one of his sons would be king forever.

For this reason, the Lubavitch movement has placed posters of their deceased head rabbi Menachem Schneerson all over Israel, with the slogan, "Baruch Haba Melech Hamashiach." "Blessed is he who comes, King Messiah." This is their messianic religious campaign to set Schneerson into office as king by the sheer force of a popular demand for him to be messiah.

While the Lubavitch movement is tragically deceived, their approach does shed light on the Matthew 23 call for the Messiah to return. Rightly seen, this is a declaration of covenant authority by the elders of Judah to inaugurate and coronate the Messiah.

This will be an act of kingdom authority to set Yeshua into His office as king over Israel and the whole world.

[**Note:** The restoration of Messianic apostolic and prophetic team ministry in Israel, as described in the previous chapter, may have a significant role to play in the spiritual authority to declare "Baruch Haba" and invite Yeshua to return as King (being a partial, New Covenant extension of the elders of Judah setting in David as king; see – **II Samuel 2:4; 19:12**).]

There has been a conflict throughout history between God and the government rulers of this world. Most leaders have usurped authority and are using their power to rebel against God. Those world leaders will have to give account before God on judgment day. Worldly government has been so evil for so long that many Christians have mistakenly come to believe that the end of the plan of God is for everyone to leave this planet and to spend eternity in the sky.

Not only is that interpretation of Scriptures incorrect, it is tragic and defeatist. It leaves the devil as having won the battle, and God relinquishing planet earth in failure. Nothing could be farther from the truth. Yeshua is returning with a heavenly army to destroy the nations that attack Jerusalem in the battle of Armageddon (**Zechariah 14:1-2, Revelation 19:11-19**). He will conquer the planet, throw the devil into the abyss, raise the dead and set up a kingdom of purity, peace and prosperity for 1,000 years.

And what will happen to all the evil governments of this world? The last part of the plan of the kingdom of God is for all the kingdoms of this world to be taken over by the saints of God and the Messiah. **"The kingdoms of the world have become the kingdom of our Lord and of His Messiah, and He shall reign forever and ever" – Revelation 11:15.** This is the final resolution of the conflict of authority between God and man.

Ultimately, there should be perfect harmony between the national government of Israel and the spiritual authority of the Church. For the first time in history, today there is a caucus and coalition in the Israeli parliament (Knesset) with Christian groups and leaders from around the world.

Yeshua is both Seed of David and Son of God (**Romans 1:3-4**); He is both King of Israel (**John 12:13**) and Head of the Church (**Ephesians 1:22**). Yeshua confirmed authority on earth to Israel by His incarnation, and authority in heaven to the Church at His ascension. In the end, all will be united.

Ephesians 1:10

In the dispensation of the fullness of times, He might gather together into one all things in Messiah, both which are in heaven and which are on the earth.

In God's eyes there is unity between His authority in heaven and earth; and, there is unity between His authority in Israel and the Church. Currently, there is division between those two spheres of authority, but Yeshua is bringing them together. At the end of God's plan, all authority will become one.

The final prayer spoken three times a day in orthodox Jewish synagogues is the "Aleinu," quoting from **Zechariah 14:9 – "It shall come to pass that YHVH will be king over all the earth. In that day YHVH will be one and his name one."**

There is another rabbinic tradition that says when a human being prays on earth with right spiritual intention, he unites the letters of the divine name YeHoVaH – the YH stand for heaven and the VH stand for earth. Through Yeshua the world will be made one, both that which is in heaven and that which is on earth. And even God's name will be made one.

Do not settle for just half the kingdom. Historically, Israel has tended to see the earthly part without the heavenly; the Church has tended to see just the heavenly without the earthly. However, Yeshua is both King of Israel and Head of the Church.

As Jewish people are coming to faith again in Yeshua, and the Church is coming to understand its covenantal connection to Israel, both are coming into unity even today. Thank God, we get the "best of both worlds" – that which is in heaven and that which is on the earth.

QUESTIONS FOR REFLECTION:

What division in the Bible provides us with a biblical pattern for understanding the split between Israel and the Church over the centuries?

What does "hamlachah" mean?

Who will do "hamlachah" with Yeshua according to Matthew 23?

What happens "in the fullness of times" at the end of God's plan?

CHAPTER 24
RULING WITH HIM

God's plan in the Bible from beginning to end contains an exciting invitation to rule and reign with Him forever. God, being God, has all power. Authority is the transfer of legal permission to use that power. God is desirous of sharing His authority and power with anyone of His beloved creatures who will show him or herself trustworthy.

From the very first moment of creating Adam and Eve, God spoke of transferring authority. It was the first sentence. It was the defining moment of destiny for human beings: to have dominion – to rule and reign with Him.

Genesis 1:26

Let Us make man in Our image and according to Our likeness; and let them have dominion over...

This opening section of the biblical plan for mankind is almost unfathomable. God has all dominion. He creates man in His image to be _like_ Him and gives him authority over the earth He has created.

At that stage there were no other human beings, so the dominion started with just the plants and the animals. But immediately God told them to multiply. We can surmise that God's initial plan included extending the Garden of Eden with more space and more population. The kingdom of God includes a huge garden of delights with lots of loving people in it. It is "a perfect world with perfect people;" "a beautiful world with beautiful people."

As the population would grow, there would be need for a society, a city, a kingdom and a system of administration, government and delegated authority. But those concepts would obviously have to wait until a later stage. (In fact we see that development of thought from a family with Abraham, to a tribe with Jacob, to a nation with Moses, to a kingdom with David, to an international empire with Solomon.)

The first social arrangement comes in the relationship between Adam and Eve in the next verse.

Genesis 1:27

So God created man in His own image; in the image of God He created him; male and female He created them.

What a simple and marvelous statement of the cooperative destiny and dominion of men and women together. They receive the creation mandate as a partnership. Authority comes from God, to Adam, to Eve, to the rest of the human race with everyone sharing and ruling together in loving harmony. Understanding our separate identities as man and woman, and of the God-ordained relationship between us, is the first step to taking dominion on the earth. The relationship between husband and wife is the first building-block of instituting divine dominion. The three-fold authority-submission between God, Adam and Eve was designed to be spread across the earth.

The male-female relationship in marriage is a partnership for cooperative destiny to rule the world (**I Peter 3:7**).

[**Note:** This verse in Genesis 1 indicates that there is a purpose in the cooperation between male and female that would not fit homo-lesbian relationships. Human beings were created to be male and female, to be in God's image, and to have dominion together. Dominion, divine destiny and the dual relationship of male and female are all woven together from the very beginning. (This is another reason why affirming homo-lesbian relationships violates God's order for blessing and authority and necessarily leads to social breakdown and spiritual darkness.)]

Although the world suffered a massive disaster by human sin and satanic rebellion, God's plan never changed. His first plan is the last plan. Our origins determine our destiny. The ultimate purpose is contained in the original proposal. While many human beings refuse to cooperate with this plan, whoever is willing to cooperate with God finds himself immediately back on the path for this dominion destiny to be fulfilled in his or her life.

From Genesis to Revelation, God's plan contains an invitation for us to rule and reign with Him. First God tells us to be "like" Him, and secondly to have "dominion" with Him. The goal of discipleship is to become "like" Him; the goal of equipping is to "rule" with Him. First we are to be conformed to the image of God in Yeshua, then we are to be trained to have dominion with Him. The first part comes by submitting to authority; the second part comes by learning how to exercise authority.

In this verse in Genesis, "let Us make man in Our image," we can already discern the central figure of the God-Man. Yeshua is the model pattern of man in the image of God, and the model of God in the likeness of man. Yeshua is the divine partner of the "We, Us and Our" in creation. To become like God means to be conformed to the image of Yeshua.

[**Note:** The word for dominion in Hebrew is very strong, from the root **"rodeh"** רדה and is found in passages such as **Psalm 110:2 – "Rule in the midst of your enemies,"** and **Psalm 144:2 – "Who subdues my people under me."**]

Let's choose the highest level of serving the Lord. When the "rich, young ruler" asked Yeshua about the minimum requirement to receive eternal life, Yeshua told him to keep the most basic of moral commandments. But then Yeshua told him that if he wanted to become "perfect," he had to give up all and to follow Him (**Matthew 19:21, Mark 10:21, Luke 18:22**).

Although the young man went away sad, Peter and the other disciples asked Yeshua, "We have given up all and followed You; what do we receive?" Yeshua said that their reward for following Him fully was to rule and reign with Him in the world to come.

Matthew 19:28

In the regeneration, when the Son of man will sit on His throne of glory, you will also sit on twelve thrones, judging the twelve tribes of Israel.

In a similar fashion, Yeshua said that anyone who is faithful even in little will have a place of authority in the world to come. There will be different levels of authority, granted according to how one is faithful in those little things in this life. Some will have more authority; some will have less. Some will rule over 10 cities, some over 5 cities.

Luke 19:17

Because you have been faithful in little, you will be ruler over ten cities.

Luke 19:19

You will be ruler over five cities.

There will not only be 12 thrones for the tribes of Israel, but another 12, presumably for other nations. **Revelation 4:4 – "Around the throne there were twenty-four thrones, and on the thrones were sitting twenty-four elders dressed in white…"**

In the worldwide kingdom of Yeshua ("The Grace Empire"), there will be myriads of government positions, leadership roles, and levels of authority. It is much more difficult for God to find and train someone in trustworthiness to fulfill one of these roles than it is simply to let the person enter the kingdom.

The positions of leadership are the minority of the population of the world to come. God is looking for more people to train and trust for such positions. Yeshua is inviting you and me to rule with Him. There seem to be very few who are willing to give up all to follow Him and to pay the price for training in trustworthiness.

When Yeshua told His disciples that they would sit on twelve thrones judging Israel, there was one person in the crowd who listened very carefully to His remarks, perhaps more carefully than anyone else. That person was "Mrs. Zebedee," the mother of John and James. Apparently, she imagined those twelve thrones and realized that no matter how they were seated, two of them would end up sitting closer to Yeshua than the other ten.

She came to Yeshua with a request.

"Please say that my two sons will sit at Your right hand and left hand in Your kingdom" – Matthew 20:21

[**On a Personal Note:** I find this request hilarious. Is it just Jewish mothers that are like this or are all mothers this way? If anyone doubted the Jewish background of the gospels, this is certainly proof enough. It is only topped by Mother Miriam (Mary) coming to Yeshua as a teenage boy and saying, "How could you do this to me? Don't you know how worried I was? (**Luke 2:48**). Oh well.]

In any case, John and James' mom really did grasp what Yeshua was saying. The kingdom is real, and there will be real positions of leadership. Yeshua went on to answer that the positions were not granted as personal favors but on the degree that the candidates would be willing to "drink the cup," to obey unto suffering and be faithful unto death (**Mark 10:38**). In the world to come, positions of authority will be granted righteously according to sacrificial love, trustworthiness and integrity.

The book of Revelation finishes what Genesis started. The description of the "New Heavens and New Earth" show paradise restored and the Garden of Eden renewed (**Revelation 21-22**). What God intended in the beginning will be fulfilled at the end. The same is true for God's destiny for mankind. The time will come for those who have been conformed to His likeness and image to take full dominion over God's creation. Yeshua as the Messiah, the King, the Christ, the image of the glory of God – He will be the ruler. In the meantime, He is inviting us to rule and reign with Him.

What is the primary quality of those who will rule and reign? – Grace and righteousness.

Romans 5:17 – "Those who receive abundance of grace and of the gift of righteousness will reign in life through Messiah Yeshua."

Where shall we reign? – On this earth.

Revelation 5:10 – "And we shall reign on the earth."

Over what will we reign? – Over all the kingdoms currently in this world's system.

Revelation 11:15 – "The kingdoms of this world have become the kingdoms of our Lord and of His Messiah, and He shall reign forever and ever."

Those who have given their lives unto death and are raised in the first resurrection, with whom will they reign? – With Yeshua.

Revelation 20:4 – "They lived and reigned with Messiah for 1,000 years."

For how much time? – For 1,000 years.

Revelation 20:5 – "They will reign with Him for 1,000 years."

Does it end after 1,000 years? – No, it will continue on into eternity.

Revelation 22:5 – "And they shall reign forever and ever."

God is inviting you and me to have forgiveness of sins, eternal life, and to rule and reign with Yeshua in His kingdom forever. Yeshua has all authority in heaven, on earth and under the earth (**Matthew 28:18, Philippians 2:9**); and, He wants to share it with us. This was our destiny from the beginning of creation

(**Genesis 1:26**). We lost it. Yeshua redeemed it. He is inviting us to rule and reign with Him.

This is what Yeshua meant when He said, "All Authority…"

QUESTIONS FOR REFLECTION:

What is the origin of the idea to "take dominion"?

Who will rule with Yeshua in the "world to come"?

How are men and women to cooperate in taking dominion?

What is the ultimate purpose for our submitting to God's authority?

SUPPLEMENTS

SUPPLEMENT 1: HEAVEN AND EARTH

The kingdom of God has aspects that are heavenly and aspects that are earthly. To understand the kingdom, we have to understand God's purpose for both heaven *and* earth. Let's review here a series of seven verses that contain the words "heaven and earth."

> **Genesis 1:1 - In the beginning God created the heavens and the earth.**

Before God created anything, He had already *planned* the kingdom, the crucifixion, the resurrection, heaven, hell, etc. What He wanted at the end was already in His thoughts from the beginning. He created the heavens and the earth because He had a *purpose* for both.

Everything He created in both heaven and earth was good, even very good. The problems entered with the rebellion of Satan and the sin of man. Ultimately, sinful and satanic things will be removed, and the heavens and the earth redeemed to their final purpose (**Romans 8:19-22**).

> **Psalm 115:16 - The heaven, even the heavens, are the Lord's; but the earth He has given to the children of men.**

This verse speaks of *delegation of authority*. The Lord has given mankind a long-term lease on planet earth. The rabbis say this is like a "two floor apartment building." God (and the angels) live in the apartment above; mankind in the apartment below. God often came to visit, like someone coming down a ladder or a staircase (**Genesis 3:8, Genesis 18:1, 21; Genesis 28:12; Exodus 3:8**). However the keys to the lower apartment were in the hands of men.

Men do not own the earth; God does. But He has given us a lease of approximately 6,000 years. For example, I live in a rented apartment. The owner has to call me and ask permission if he wants to visit. The keys are in my hands.

> **Isaiah 65:17 - Behold I create new heavens and a new earth; and the former shall not be remembered or come to mind.**

God promises to create a new heavens and earth. This does not mean that the current universe will go out of existence, but that God will *restore, renew* and *redeem*. In the context of Isaiah 65, we see that the earth will be purified, but that the natural processes will continue, though greatly and supernaturally improved.

The difference is like from the time before the flood of Noah to after the flood of Noah, yet even more so (**II Peter 3:5-12**). When the book of Revelation (chapters 21-22) refers to New Heavens and Earth, it is giving additional revelation about this passage in Isaiah 65. As his custom, John gives spiritual insight to what is written in the other Hebrew prophets. He is adding a dimension to what was already said and not doing away with it.

Isaiah gave the earthly perspective; John the heavenly. We need to see it from both angles.

> **Matthew 5:3, 5 - Blessed are the poor in spirit, for theirs is the kingdom of heaven. Blessed are the meek, for they shall inherit the earth.**

There are many injustices in the world today. Since God is both *powerful* and *moral*, He will remove the unjust elements. Those who are pure in heart will then take over what is here. Religions which do not understand the nature of the God of the Bible believe that pure hearted people will just leave this place for eternity. They do not see how God could bring justice, remove the wicked, reward the righteous and restore the earth.

Therefore, they abandon God's good creation and leave for some other mystical, non-physical, unidentified place. This type of "escapist" theology or an eternal separation of physical and spiritual is not according to the biblical world view, in my opinion. The Bible describes God as a benevolent Creator who unites both the spiritual and physical in a restored, renewed and perfected universe.

> **Matthew 6:10 - Your kingdom come; Your will be done on earth as it is in heaven.**

The kingdom of God has an *origin*, a *direction* and a *destination*. It starts in heaven. It comes toward us. It eventually takes over the earth. The kingdom of God comes in stages. It grows from small to big; it grows from inside to outside (Matthew 13:31-33). The kingdom of God is an invasion, not an evacuation (albeit a gracious invasion, but an invasion nonetheless).

Yeshua left for a time to establish the authority of His kingdom, but is coming again to rule and reign (Luke 19:12). Some people understand salvation only as fire insurance and a helicopter ticket (go to heaven instead of hell). Yet the kingdom of God is also an ownership certificate and a government constitution (redeeming the planet and ruling in the world to come).

Although the statement in the Lord's prayer about God's will being done on earth and His kingdom coming to earth is perhaps the most oft spoken prayer in the world, it doesn't seem that most people really mean what they are saying.

It is worth noting that the Jewish prayer book ends *every* service with the prayer, **"Aleinu"** עֲלֵינוּ which includes the words **"tikkun olam"** תִּיקוּן עוֹלָם which means "to restore (or repair) the world."

Matthew 28:18 - All authority has been given to Me in heaven and on earth.

Yeshua is both God and man; therefore He has authority on both heaven and earth. His authority in heaven stems from His divinity – His authority on earth from His humanity. The gospel is effective because of His *dual nature* and *dual authority*. He came from heaven and was born into a physical body on this earth. He was physically raised from the dead. He ascended into heaven. He will return some day as He ascended (Acts 1:11), and His feet will once again stand on the Mount of Olives (Zechariah 14:4).

Not to affirm Yeshua's actual return to earth and a literal millennial reign is to mock the physical pain He suffered on the cross and to deny the purpose of the bodily resurrection. I am perplexed as to how difficult it is for many to see the literal fulfillment of the biblical promises concerning the millennial reign of Messiah.

Ephesians 1:10 - In the dispensation of the fullness of the times, He might gather together in one all things in Messiah, both which are in heaven and on earth – in Him (Yeshua).

Please compare this verse to **Colossians 1:16** which states that *all* things in heaven *and* earth were created for Yeshua and through Yeshua.

Today unfortunately, there is still a separation between things in heaven and on earth. But that is not God's will. Ultimately all things both in heaven and on earth will be brought together through Yeshua the Messiah. That was His mission – to *unite heaven and earth*.

SUPPLEMENT 2: KURIOS

The historical events of the Tanakh (Old Testament) end with the book of Nehemiah around 440 BC. The last book of the Tanakh to be written and edited was Chronicles. In I Chronicles 3 there is a genealogical list that continues some 10 generations after Zerubavel, which would date it to approximately 350 BC. In 333 BC Alexander the Great conquered the Middle East and imposed Greek culture and language on the people living there.

Between 280 and 130 BC, Greek-speaking rabbinic scholars translated the Tanakh into Greek, known as the Septuagint. This became the most reliable version of the Tanakh and is the version quoted in the New Covenant. In the Holy Land, a dynamic tension developed between the international Greek culture and the local Hebrew-Aramaic culture. This tension at times worked for good and at times for bad.

The Maccabean revolt started in 166 BC, overthrew the Greeks, and the Judean Hashmonean Empire lasted until the area was conquered by Rome under Pompeus in 63 BC. By the time Yeshua was born, the Holy Land was ruled by Herod (Idomean-Greek Jewish convert), who was appointed under the auspices of the Roman Empire.

The apostle Paul (Saul) was educated in both Jewish and Greek studies. The dual use of His name with Saul and Paul may reflect the divine commission to take the gospel from the Hebrew world to the Greek international community. The authoritative text of the full Bible is written in Hebrew in the Tanakh and Greek in the New Covenant.

The tension between Hebrew and Greek continued into the early community of faith. On Pentecost morning, the 120 Hebrew-speaking disciples preached the gospel to a crowd of 3,000 people of primarily international background (**Acts 2:9-11**). The number of disciples grew among both Hebrew and Greek speakers.

Acts 6:1 - As the number of disciples grew, the Greek-speaking Jews began to complain against the Hebrew speakers, because their widows were being neglected.

The clash of the two culture groups caused problems in communication, finances, and administration. A committee was appointed from among the Greek speakers to make sure the logistics were being handled properly (**Acts 6:5**). The identity issues continued with the development of the international church (ecclesia). The order of the gospel is to the Jew first, then the Greek

(**Romans 1:16, 2:10**); and yet, Jews and Greeks have the same spiritual standing before God (**Galatians 3:28**).

We experience similar tensions in the Messianic congregations here in Israel, as we are a Hebrew-speaking nation, yet the number of non-Hebrew speaking new immigrants and international guests is larger than the Hebrew-speaking core. There is a perfect balance between the universal international aspects of the faith and the Israelite covenantal aspects of the faith.

At the end of the Tanakh period, people still pronounced the name YHVH. By the time of the Gospel texts, the name was not used. In that same "intertestamental" period (approximately in which the Tanakh was translated into Greek), the Jewish people stopped speaking the name of YHVH. Ultimately, the pronunciation was forgotten and forbidden. Instead of YHVH, the term "Adonai" began to be used, which is the plural form of the word "lord." In the Septuagint, the name YHVH was translated to the term "Kurios," which also means "lord."

So at approximately the same period in history, the name YHVH stopped being used and was replaced by *Adonai* in Hebrew and *Kurios* in Greek. Depending on the context, both terms can have the composite meanings "LORD, Lord, and lord." By the time of Yeshua, there is no YHVH in use, but only *Adonai* and *Kurios*. All of the citations of YHVH in the Septuagint and New Covenant translate YHVH to *Kurios*. *Kurios* means *Adonai* and YHVH.

Amazingly, in the New Covenant, Yeshua is referred to as *Kurios*. This can be seen as calling Him "LORD, Lord or lord." Calling Yeshua *Kurios* is like calling Him *Adonai*. It is a bold and unavoidable declaration of both His human and divine authority. Yeshua is *Kurios-Adonai*. This declaration of faith was shocking both to Hebrew speakers and to Greek. To call Yeshua *Lord-Kurios-Adonai* is an explosive breakthrough in the history of faith, religion, and revelation.

SUPPLEMENT 3: REWARDS IN HEAVEN

After the Millennial kingdom, from the time of the Second Resurrection and the New Creation, the ultimate destiny of every man is either eternal bliss in paradise or eternal torment in the lake of fire. There is no middle ground. If there is eternal existence, and if there is absolute justice, there are no other possible options.

> **Revelation 20:15 - Anyone not found written in the book of life was cast into the lake of fire.**

The difference between these two final options is what motivates us to preach the gospel. Everyone will be resurrected eternally, either for blessing or punishment (**Daniel 12:2, Isaiah 66:24**).

Yet Yeshua also talked of different levels of reward and punishment. When He taught on prayer, fasting, and charity, Yeshua said that if we do these things with a pure heart, then we would receive reward in the world to come. If on the other hand, our motives were not pure, our reward would be canceled.

> **Matthew 6:4, 6, 18 - Your Father who sees in secret will reward you openly.**

The people He is talking about here are "believers." This is not a difference between being damned or saved, but rather a difference as to what reward you will receive in paradise. Each time we do righteous deeds with a pure heart, we store up for ourselves reward in heaven. To the degree that we act hypocritically, our rewards are nullified.

Since each action has a cumulative reward, every person will receive a different level of reward in the world to come.

In order to be saved, we must receive forgiveness of sins by faith in Yeshua's sacrifice for us on the cross. Anyone who rejects the saving grace of Yeshua must stand in judgment (**Mark 16:16**). He who does believe in Yeshua passes out of this judgment and receives salvation (**John 5:24**). God does not seek to punish anyone, but he who rejects the offer of eternal life is in effect condemned of his own (**John 3:18**).

In the sense of being condemned, a true believer in Yeshua is not "judged." However, there is another meaning to the word "judge," which is not referring to damnation or salvation, but to reward and punishment. In this sense every believer will be judged.

II Corinthians 5:10 - For we must all appear before the judgment seat of Christ, that each one may receive the things done in the Body, according to what he has done, whether good or bad.

This statement of the Apostle Paul was made to born-again, spirit-filled believers. He included himself in this judgment when he said, "we."

If all saved people will live eternally in paradise, and if paradise is such a perfect place, how could there be different levels of reward there? Let us examine four areas:

1. Position of authority - The world to come is a real society. Everyone will have a job. There will be positions of leadership and government.

> **Luke 19:17 - "Well done, good servant; because you were faithful in a very little, have authority over ten cities."**

> **Luke 19:19 - "You also be over five cities."**

> **Luke 19:24 - "Take the portion away from him, and give it to him who has ten."**

Some people will have authority over thousands (like ten cities). Others will have lesser positions (like five cities). Others will have jobs with no authority at all (like the one whose portion was taken away).

2. Magnitude of Glory - In the world to come, we will live in resurrected bodies. These bodies will be glorified, meaning that they will shine with light like stars by the power of God. But like the stars, not every person's body will shine with the same degree of glory.

> **I Corinthians 15:39-42 - There are celestial bodies and terrestrial bodies; but the glory of the celestial is one, and the glory of the terrestrial is another. There is one glory of the sun, another glory of the moon, and another glory of the stars; for one star differs from another in glory. So also is the resurrection of the dead.**

The difference between our bodies now and our bodies after the resurrection will be like the difference between the earth (which doesn't shine) and a star (which does shine). However, there is another difference. "For one star differs from another star in glory (vs. 41)." Just as there is a difference in the magnitude of light coming from each star, so will it be in the resurrection. Each person's body will have a different degree of light shining from it - some more, some less.

3. Proximity to Yeshua - While all true believers will be physically present in the world to come, and while everyone will have access to meet Yeshua, not everyone will have the same proximity to Him on a day-to-day basis. John and James' mother once came asking a request from Yeshua.

> **Matthew 20:21 - "Grant that these two sons of mine may sit, one Your right hand and the other on the left, in Your kingdom."**

While Yeshua could not grant her request, He did affirm the fact that there will be a certain "assigned seating" arrangement at events in the kingdom of God. As a citizen of Israel, I have general access to see the Prime Minister. However, only those on his immediate staff can meet with him every day. Only those with higher positions in the government can easily obtain an appointment with him. The degree of one's accessibility to Yeshua is considered a great reward in the kingdom of God.

4. Heavenly "Treasure" - Sometimes people say, concerning money, "You can't take it with you." That is not entirely true. Just as there are banks on earth, there is some type of "banking" system in heaven.

> **Matthew 6:20 - Lay up for yourselves treasures in heaven, where neither moth nor rust destroys and thieves do not break in and steal.**

You make a deposit in your account in heaven by giving money to others. I don't know if there is an actual "currency" in the world to come. However, there must be some kind of "treasure" or what Yeshua said would be meaningless. Whatever that heavenly "treasure" is there must be different degrees to which it can be "stored up." There will be different quantitative rewards in the world to come.

When referring to rewards according to our works, we must remember that God looks at the heart and not at the outward appearance. Many things that seem to be great works in the eyes of men are nothing in the eyes of God. And many deeds that seem to be worthless in the eyes of men are of great value to God.

Yeshua said of the poor widow who gave two small coins that she gave more than the great sums of money given by the wealthy (**Luke 21:3**). In what sense did she give more? Her gift was greater than the others in its deposit in the heavenly bank because it took more faith and love to give it.

So it is with many other kinds of works. A great evangelist may be motivated by worldly ambition and even though he was used by God to save thousands, he may receive little reward in the world to come (**Phil. 1:15-16**). Another may only "succeed" in giving one cup of water, but thereby receive the same reward as a prophet (**Matt. 10:41-42**)! If you are just faithful in the very little thing that God has put in your path, you may receive an enormous reward in the world to come.

Some people think that it is unbiblical and selfish to be motivated by rewards in the world to come. But that is not true. It is wrong to be motivated by the honor of man rather than the honor of God (**John 5:44**), and by the carnal rewards of this life rather than the eternal rewards of the world to come (**Hebrews 11:25-26**).

In fact, the Bible says that we cannot even please God unless we believe that He will reward those who diligently seek Him (**Hebrews 11:6**). Behavioral science correctly teaches that rewards encourage certain behavior and punishments discourage. Yet the very concept of reward and punishment, both temporal and eternal, comes from God.

There will also be certain punishments among those who receive eternal life. How can there be punishments when a person is saved? Any sin that is repented of by a believer is atoned for by the blood of Yeshua and erased. Yet sin that is not repented of will receive punishment. Five of the seven churches in the book of Revelation received rebukes from Yeshua. He was not speaking primarily of their losing salvation, but of losing their rewards. By punishment here I do not mean eternal damnation, but rather temporary chastisement.

The Bible speaks of Yeshua having a "rod" that comes out of His mouth. By this I understand that the primary chastisement of believers in the world to come will not be torment by fire nor even physical beatings, but rather a firm and honest rebuke by Jesus, which will be witnessed by millions in the Day of Judgment.

Yeshua will not give us false compliments or flattery. If we have disobeyed Him, failed to fulfill our destiny, or simply led a carnal lifestyle, He will speak bluntly and authoritatively to the point. I would rather receive a thousand lashes than to hear a word of disapproval from the lips of Yeshua on "that day."

> **Luke 12:47-48 - That servant who knew his master's will, and did not prepare himself or do according to his will, shall be beaten with many stripes. But he who did not know, yet committed things deserving of stripes, shall be beaten with few.**

Receiving a few more or a few less beatings could not apply to someone who would spend eternity in the lake of fire. There are degrees of responsibility and commitment in the kingdom of God. We are held responsible for what we know. The level of punishment is meted out accordingly.

So in the kingdom of God there will be different levels of reward and punishment. Some will receive more. Some will receive less. Some will receive nothing at all.

I Corinthians 3:14-15 - **"If anyone's work that he has built on [the foundation which is Jesus Christ] endures, he will receive a reward. If anyone's work is burned, he will suffer loss; but he himself will be saved."**

We are saved through faith in Yeshua. That is our foundation. With that foundation a person builds his life with a quality like gold or silver, wood or hay. According to the life we live, we will be rewarded or not rewarded; we will be praised or rebuked.

SUPPLEMENT 4: WISDOM AND THE FEAR OF GOD

Wisdom is the ability to know what is the right thing to do. Obviously, before we can do the right thing, we have to know what it is. From God's point of view, if He sees that someone really wants to do the right thing, He will let them understand (**John 7:17**). If someone wants to know wisdom just for the sake of intellectual curiosity or pride, then God has no interest in revealing to him what the right thing is (**Matthew 11:25**).

If we do want to do the right thing and don't know what it is, then we are invited by God to ask Him; He will be delighted to show us (**Ephesians 1:17, James 1:5**).

The first part of seeking wisdom goes a bit against our natural inclinations. We know that the beginning of wisdom is the "Fear of YHVH" (**Psalm 111:10, Proverbs 1:7**). Fear of YHVH comes from the knowledge that God punishes sin and that we have all sinned.

It's as if someone is travelling on a road, and then checks the map and realizes he is heading in the wrong direction. He has to stop, reevaluate and turn around. That is not easy. That is called "repentance." Repentance is the first step to obeying God.

Fear of God can also be defined as "moral courage." Yeshua defined the fear of YHVH as fearing the punishment of hell after death (**Luke 12:5**). That is the bottom line in the fear of God.

Yet in that same passage, Yeshua spoke 7 times of not fearing any man, need or circumstances (**Luke 12:4, 7, 11, 22** (about being anxious), **26** (about being anxious), **29** (about worry), **32**). The fear of God eliminates every other kind of fear in life. To have the fear of God is to be totally fearless of every danger.

The Bible describes the fear of God as the "beginning" of wisdom. Yet sometimes the first becomes the last. It seems that for many, the true fear of God is the very last part of wisdom to be understood. Let us diligently seek for the fear of YHVH (**Jeremiah 5:24, Job 28:28**). Yeshua had a regular habit of seeking the fear of God in early morning prayer through tears and groaning (**Mark 1:35, Hebrews 5:7**).

When we realize that God punishes evil, then we can:

1. Stop doing things wrong ourselves

2. Not be afraid of evil in others

3. Fight evil in the world.

Thus the fear of the Lord gives us the moral courage to stand up against evil even though it is scary to do so (and of course after having repented ourselves). The fear of the Lord includes an inner motivation to confront evil.

Proverbs 8:13 – The fear of YHVH is to hate evil.

Unfortunately, most of us are active in being selfish and passive in standing against evil. However, the fear of God gives us an active power to fight against evil – first in ourselves and then in others. It is said that all that is needed for evil to triumph is for the good to do nothing. The fear of YHVH provides the moral courage to fight evil.

SUPPLEMENT 5: OIL AND PRESS

The name Gethsemane in Hebrew is **"Gat Sh'manim,"** גת שמנים meaning "Oil Press." It is the place where olives are brought and crushed; the skin and pit are strained and separated. The result is pure olive oil. Oil is a consistent biblical symbol for the anointing of the Holy Spirit. It may well be that Yeshua chose Gat Sh'manim with this name on purpose.

There are a variety of uses of the image of oil throughout Scriptures, often referring to the anointing and power of the Holy Spirit. The anointing oil brings protection, provision, and prosperity (**Psalm 23:5**), wisdom and authority to rule (**I Samuel 16:13**), joy (**Psalm 45:7, Hebrews 1:9**), healing and deliverance (**Mark 6:13, James 5:14**), light and revelation (**Exodus 25:6, I John 2:27, Revelation 3:18**), ability to preach and prophecy (**Isaiah 61:1**), intimacy in worship (**Song of Solomon 1:3, Matthew 25:3, Mark 14:3**), and much more.

There is a dynamic relationship between the oil and the press. They are opposites that balance out one another. At Gat Sh'manim Yeshua embraced the cross. He forced His will to submit (**Matthew 26:39**). It is a place of darkness, depression, and difficulty (**Matthew 26:37**). It is a place of self-denial (**Matthew 16:24**); a place to be crushed; to obey unto death; to be tested; to pass through humiliation and suffering; to intercede to the point of blood, sweat, and tears.

The oil certainly seems more attractive than the oil press. Yet there is no oil without the press. The oil is produced at the oil press. There is no other way to produce true oil. On the other hand, the purpose of the press is to obtain the oil. To suffer in obedience without obtaining that oil is not according to the heart of God. The press is for the oil. The oil comes from the press.

SUPPLEMENT 6: CREATION AND DOMINION

By Youval Yanay

Recently our team went through an extended workshop on communication skills by working together with a Christian professional horse trainer and coach. The treatment with the horses brought us to deeper understanding of ourselves and our interactions with one another.

Genesis 1:26 - Then God said, "Let Us make man in Our image, according to Our likeness; let them have dominion over the fish of the sea, over the birds of the air, and over the cattle, over all the earth..."

This verse has two parts. First, we are made in God's image. Secondly, we are to rule over the animals. The first part causes and enables the second part to take place. God is the perfect ruler over the creation. He knows His creation, upholds it, and works in harmony with it.

Taking dominion over the creation means to be over and above the creation – to understand more, to love more, and to be more confident. That is our rightful position as being made in God's image. It does not mean to abuse, curse, or harm God's creation, nor to be alienated and separated from it. In order to take dominion correctly, God gives us His own image and likeness.

God has subjected and submitted the creation to us. The welfare of the planet is dependent upon our ability to fulfill our destiny as God's children (**Romans 8:19-22**). Our successfully or unsuccessfully taking dominion over the earth determines the condition of the planet.

Likewise, the condition of the creation reflects our being made in the creator's image. Our ability to take dominion correctly over the creation reflects the degree to which we are fulfilling our calling in God's image. Dealing with creation is a test of our own image and spiritual condition. How do we appear as reflected in creation's mirror?

Are we in the image and likeness of God? Are we in right relationship to God's creation? To what degree are we upholding, understanding and ruling the creation? By seeing the reaction of the creation to us, our own hearts are exposed as to whether we are fulfilling God's first commandment and mandate.

SUPPLEMENT 7: THE GENEROSITY GOSPEL

Sometimes I am asked if I believe in the "Prosperity" gospel. What I believe in is the "Generosity" gospel. There is a divine revelation of God's desire to bless His people in every way, including financially. The issue of blessing can be seen at the first covenant of God with Abraham:

Genesis 12:2 – I will bless you.

Genesis 12:3 – In you all the families of the earth will be blessed.

We are blessed so that we can be a blessing to others. The issue here is the intention of the heart. We desire to be blessed IN ORDER TO bless others. Every blessing of God also contains its own temptation and the moral test to steward it properly. Solomon was blessed financially, but in the end, he was lured away from the Lord.

[Notice that in this passage the financial blessing of God is connected to the restoration of Israel (**Genesis 12:1 - "Go to a land which I will show you."**) and to world evangelism (**verse 3 - "All the families of the earth"**).]

There is a perfect balance to the word of God (a two edged sword). If we encourage people with the blessing of prosperity, we also have to warn them of the danger of greed. Greed is so dangerous that it can result in the type of sin that would bring eternal punishment (**Luke 12:16-21, Luke 16:19-26**). The problem is not so much in what is preached by "prosperity" teachers, but in what they are not teaching. If you teach just half a message, even if it is true, then it becomes misleading.

This fault can be found on either side. If we teach only on God's will to prosper financially without the character issues involved, people will ultimately become indulgent and greedy. Some preachers try to attract people to give to their ministry, or to come to their church, by giving a message that is basically an appeal to the lusts of this world.

However, if we do not teach God's will to prosper, the people will remain largely unfruitful and unbelieving. Many times people complain about those "prosperity" teachers, and then in the next breath they complain about their own lack of finances. Yeshua's teaching is stunningly balanced and stunningly simple:

Luke 6:38 – Give and it will be given to you.

This is an example of "measure opposite measure," the law of equal action and reaction. I would summarize the basic principles of finances in Scripture this way: **INTEGRITY + GENEROSITY = PROSPERITY**

Integrity includes hard work and honesty. Integrity demands paying taxes. If we are to pay all our taxes, give decent wages to our employees, provide for our children's education, we will quickly find that we need a lot more money than we ever imagined. Therefore, integrity demands prosperity.

If we want to help the poor, strengthen the body of Messiah, and spread the gospel, we will need even more provision. Thus, generosity demands prosperity.

Although Yeshua taught on the perfect balance of generosity and prosperity (Luke 6:38 above), He also taught that one is better than the other.

Acts 20:35 – It is more blessed to give than to receive.

We will be judged, not by what we have, but by what we give (**Luke 12:15; 21:3, Acts 10:4**). When we receive something in this world, it is temporary. When we give, the fruit lasts forever.

We are to give no thought to our own provision (**Matthew 6:25**) – that is worry; nor to our own prosperity (**Romans 13:14**) – that is greed. We are to be focused on bearing MUCH fruit for the kingdom of God (**John 15:8**) – that takes generosity; and His righteousness (**Matthew 6:33**) – that takes integrity.

Generosity is central to the plan of God. (**John 3:16 – God so loved the world that He gave…**) True faith in God will produce generosity of heart. Generosity may be seen both as character and as charisma.

Character means the personality qualities of God. We are to **"give to all who ask"** (**Luke 6:30**), so that we will become **"sons of the Most High"** (**Luke 6:35**). That is our reward – to be like Yeshua. God has great generosity of heart. I want to be like Him. Therefore I want to develop generosity in all things including finances.

Giving is also a charisma, a supernatural gift of the Holy Spirit. In speaking of financial giving, Paul said, **"As you abound in faith, speech, knowledge, diligence and love, see that you abound in this grace (charisma) as well"** – **II Corinthians 8:7**. So we are to grow in generosity as both a fruit and a gift of the Spirit.

Just as we are passionate to worship and share the word, so should we be passionate in our giving. In the first century community of faith, there was supernatural giving. Apostolic restoration will include apostolic generosity. The businessmen were as much a part of the Great Commission as the prophets and evangelists:

Acts 4:34-35 – All who were possessors of lands or houses sold them, and brought the proceeds of the things that were sold, and laid them at the apostles' feet.

This money was used for the needs of the congregation and for the world mission. These saints understood their destiny together to change the entire world (remember **Genesis 12:2-3**). That vision was so exciting that people wanted to give everything to be part of it. The same fire of Pentecost (Shavuot) revival and world evangelism also made them "burn" with excitement to give. Their supernatural giving was "vision motivated."

SUPPLEMENT 8: RELIGIOUS LIBERTY
By Daniel Juster

In all ancient cultures, religious order and governmental authority were tied together. The gods of one's tribe were tied to ancestors, to the chief of the tribe, and to the elders. They were totally intertwined. The idea of any separation was not on the horizon of human consciousness. Some Greek philosophers questioned and sometimes even mocked the common religious ideas of their day. However, the people were still expected to show loyalty to the city or polis by participating in temple rights and sacrifices. It was part of civic duty.

Rome practiced a high degree of toleration for different sects and beliefs, but only within limits. As the cult of the emperor became normative, the peoples of the empire were expected to engage in religious ceremony acknowledging the lordship and divinity of Caesar. The fact that Judaism was given liberty from the cult of the empire was quite amazing. They were only required to offer a sacrifice for (rather than to) the emperor.

Liberty and Ancient Israel

Ancient Israel was a theocracy and was not enjoined to religious liberty. All Israelites were required to be loyal to the God of Abraham, Isaac and Jacob. Sojourners and strangers in their midst were to show respect to the God of Israel and not engage in foreign practices on Israeli soil. The prophets of Baal were killed in the days of Elijah. False prophets and even entire cities that practiced idolatry were to be destroyed.

The Origins of Religious Liberty

So what is the origin of religious liberty? It began, I believe, with the first century community of faith with the apostles of Yeshua and became a foundation of early Christianity. In **Acts 5:28-29**, the religious authorities commanded the Apostles to not preach and teach in the name of Yeshua. Instead, the Apostles declared that they had to obey God rather than man, and that they could not but speak what they had seen and heard. Their refusal to accept the command of the Sanhedrin asserted their right to uphold their convictions of conscience above and against the authorities. Their appeal to God's authority over the Sanhedrin demonstrated that the ruling was unjust and therefore any persecution for disobedience to the ruling was unjust.

When "the way" spread to the nations and included Gentiles, this assertion of religious liberty became more pronounced. Followers of Yeshua declared that He was Lord, a challenge to the very idea that Caesar was Lord. Christians in the Roman Empire thus asserted two freedoms of conscience: to declare Yeshua is Lord and to deny that Lordship to Caesar. They also asserted that their persecution was unjust.

Daniel Boyarin, an Orthodox Jewish, yet liberal scholar at Berkeley, California, argues that our idea of religion as a system of beliefs, ethics and practices that a person can choose from among a number of options, was an invention of early Christianity. Eventually Judaism as well was redefined. For almost 300 years Christians asserted this right of religious liberty and freedom of conscience. We do not have any evidence as to how they thought the state should be organized were their faith to triumph.

The Origins of a State Church

When Constantine became a Christian, sincerely or feigned, he made Christianity the preferred religion of the empire. Other religions were still tolerated. However, 50 years later Christianity became the official state religion and other religions were suppressed. Not until the 17th century do we find a state that practiced true religious liberty.

The Modern Origin of Religious Liberty

In the 17th century, the Baptist pastor Roger Williams surveyed the results of European religious wars and the violation of conscience in Puritan colonies. He wrote many tracts against the wars and bloody persecutions. For Williams, there was to be a separation of civil government from church government. Williams founded Rhode Island, the first state to enshrine genuine religious freedom. For Williams the conscience must not be constrained, because true religion requires freedom of conscience, including the right to seek to persuade others of one's beliefs or lack thereof. This was revolutionary.

Williams and the founding fathers of the United States did not interpret this separation to mean that the State would not acknowledge God's basic law and their accountability to God. It was an institutional separation. It was assumed that a Judeo-Christian framework would be foundational for the state. The law provided limits to liberty in such matters as for example, child sacrifice, perverted sexual practices, prostitution, and child sexual abuse (all of which happens in some religions).

It was difficult for societies to come to the view of Williams. They saw the intertwining of church and state as necessary for social order. Furthermore, when toleration was finally granted in the United Kingdom, there was still a favored state church. It was only recently that the Roman Catholic Church officially affirmed genuine religious freedom as taught in the tradition of Roger Williams.

Religious Liberty Today

Today, we live in a difficult situation where true religious freedom is not defended. We see this in the attempt to blame the evangelists for the persecution they receive in other cultures. We see this among the Hindus who fear the loss of their religious caste system. However, the greatest religious coercion and violation of human rights is in the Muslim world where true religious freedom does not exist in a single Muslim country. In all these cases, loyalty to tribe and caste supersedes a person's right to search for the truth and their right to persuade others. I believe it is crucial for young adults to have the right to search and to confirm the beliefs and practices that their parents and congregation have conveyed to them. Some are so sure that they do not know such a need, but those who do search and confirm will have a strong faith. The standards we support are written in the Universal Declaration of Human Rights.

Liberty and the Jewish Community

Our situation in the Jewish community is also one where coercion seeks to restrict conscience. We see this in the Israeli Interior Ministry that attempts to block Messianic Jews from citizenship. We see it in harassment from the same department by withholding passports and services. The ultra-orthodox have demonstrated against congregations, sometimes with vandalism and violence. One individual bombed a Messianic Jewish home, terribly injuring a young person. The idea that the family and community will reject you for your beliefs is a type of religious coercion that should have no place in the modern world.

SUPPLEMENT 9: EXCEPTION TO THE RULE

After 3,000 years of being a chosen, holy people (**Exodus 19:6**) but without knowing our own Messiah, we Jews seem to know that we have a special calling but don't know exactly why. We even pray, "Blessed are You our God who has chosen us from all the nations."

In addition, we received God's absolute moral standard in the Torah at Sinai, but have never fulfilled it as it should be (**Jeremiah 31:32**). But we certainly affirm the concept that everyone has to obey the Law. So we have these two deeply engrained subconscious assumptions: we know that we are chosen from other people, and we know that everyone has to obey "the rules."

Perhaps because of this background, we Jews in Israel (secular, religious and Messianic alike) tend to have a strange psychological syndrome I call "exception to the rule." It goes like this:

Rules are important. Everyone has to obey the rules. Anyone who doesn't obey the rules should be rebuked and punished. In fact I must go and rebuke them for not obeying the rules. However, I am a special case because of the importance of my calling. I am an exception to the rules; the rules apply to everyone else, but not to me.

[Perhaps this psychological dysfunction occurs in people of other ethnic and religious backgrounds as well. In fact, perhaps you may even have noticed this tendency in yourself, focusing on what others are doing wrong, yet seeing yourself as a special exception to the rule.]

SUPPLEMENT 10: SPIRITUAL INHERITANCE

By *Tod McDowell and Don Finto*

Tod's Story:

There are blessings, anointings and destiny that are passed down through family lines and generations both physically and spiritually. Many times the son or daughter does not provide a "landing pad" of faith and initiative to receive and walk out these gifts and callings that God has passed down. It is our imperative actively to seek, knock and ask for these blessings to be manifest in and through our lives (**Matthew 7:7-8**).

When I met Don Finto, I was praying and preparing to start a new ministry on my own. I had a name, a website domain and a staff of 12 people along with a council of leaders that were supporting me. When God led me to "walk with Don," I had no idea where I was headed. I traveled with him when our schedules permitted.

After several months, my wife Rachel challenged me to be more committed and connected. So I began a proactive engagement of pursuing mentoring and fathering. It was humbling at first to admit that I needed a spiritual father at the age of thirty-six years old. I had been leading out in missions work on my own with seasonal leaders for fifteen years already.

At one point the following year I was in Israel with Don and we met with Asher Intrater. He noticed that I was walking with Don like a son to him, but didn't know what my commitment was. He asked me, "Are you the spiritual son that is going to carry on Don's legacy and embrace and expand his inheritance?" It so happened that I had spoken with Rachel earlier that day and we had agreed; so I was ready to answer with a "Yes, indeed."

This shifted my focus from wanting to start my own ministry to wanting to invest in the legacy that Don had built for many years. This focus steered me away from a "self-focus" pursuit in what I wanted to do in ministry and caused me to submit myself to embracing what Don had already done, and how I could expand that through my own gifting, talents and vision.

I believe we only have as much as authority in our lives as we are submitted to authority. I know that I am much more protected and safe now that I have submitted to Don's spiritual authority. I have never felt controlled or manipulated by Don, but only released and championed.

He endorsed me with our board of directors at Caleb Company to become the new executive director, taking his place as the "on the ground" leader. This did not change my relational submission to his authority in my life. I call him whenever I need counsel and still share my heart secrets with him on a daily and weekly basis as we are able.

Don's story:

When David and Emma Rudolph came back from having leased their first apartment in Israel, Emma was especially moved in the Spirit about having a home back in the land of her inheritance, returning from hundreds of years of exile. When she said that, I had a Holy Spirit encounter about a stored up intended inheritance in each of our bloodlines waiting to be deposited on a willing recipient. I realized that my life is all about providing a landing pad for the Holy Spirit.

In my closing years at Belmont Church, God touched **Numbers 8:24-25** with revelation for my life. God told Moses to tell Aaron that the Levites were to do the actual ministry from their 25th to their 50th year after which they were to assist the people doing it. I understood God to be telling me that the primary role of my life was no longer about my own ministry, but about empowering next generations.

Asher once told me that he did not want my spiritual legacy to die, and that he would do whatever had to be done to make sure that legacy would continue. At one point, we even brought our databases into sync. When he saw Tod's and my father/son role, he called us together and told Tod, "If you do not want this inheritance, then I'm not giving it to you. But if you do, you can have the first born rights and the double inheritance." Tod's response was, "I want both!"

Tod is taking my inheritance to a new level. Our relationship to Heidi Baker and Iris Ministries, with the underground church in China, in Finland, in Mexico, and many other places, all came through Tod and Rachel, not through me. This is a great blessing to me.

A true father will always rejoice in a son or daughter's godliness and success. My ceiling must be his floor. He wants the "family business" to prosper, because he will inherit the whole business when I go on.

SUPPLEMENT 11: RECOVERING THE APOSTOLIC COMMISSION

Our faith in Messiah Yeshua includes taking part in a grand vision and challenge to change the world. This "great commission" was given to the original Apostles and disciples right before Yeshua ascended into heaven. That commission includes making disciples (**Matthew 28:19**), preaching the gospel (**Mark 16:15**), and also "restoring the kingdom to Israel."

Acts 1:6 – "Will you at this time restore the kingdom to Israel?"

Acts 1:8 – You will receive power when the Holy Spirit comes upon you; and be witnesses of Me in Jerusalem, all Judea and Samaria, even unto the ends of the earth.

Many people today speak of restoring the Jewish roots of the faith. However, those roots are more profound than the cultural elements of food and festivals. Recovering the original apostolic commission is a central aspect of the restoration of the so-called "Jewish Roots." Restoring the Messianic remnant in Israel today includes recovering the kingdom vision of the original Apostles.

The Messianic remnant and the Apostolic commission should go hand in hand!

Isaac went back to dig the wells of Abraham; he called them by the names that his father called them (**Genesis 26:18**). The wells and the names were tools to get back the water that his father had found. Our Messianic Jewish attempt to redig the "wells" of our forefathers, by understanding the cultural, geographic and linguistic context of the Scriptures, has the goal of getting back to the spiritual waters of salvation and rivers of revival that our "fathers" – the apostles – had found.

The ancient covenants had accompanying signs to help "remember" the covenants. What we were supposed to remember is God's faithfulness to fulfill the content of the covenants. The prophecies are promises from God. The covenants remind us of the faithfulness of God.

Jewish culture, Israeli geography and Hebrew language are symbols and sign posts to find the treasures to get back to the kingdom glory and power of our forefathers. They are tools to understand the mysteries hidden long ago in the words of Scripture (**Romans 16:25-26**). We want to use the road map in order to find the treasure laid by the apostles and prophets.

Peter, John and Paul are just as much our "Jewish" fathers as Abraham, Isaac and Jacob. (The apostles all had two names – one in Greek and one in Hebrew, since they were all bilingual and bicultural. They used their Greek names in international venues and their Hebrew names within Israel.)

Some of the "Abrahamic" wells that the Apostles dug were: the Messianic kingdom on earth (**Acts 1:3**), the baptism of the Holy Spirit (**Acts 1:5**), world evangelism (**Acts 1:8**), a literal Second Coming (**Acts 1:11**), world revival in the end times (**Acts 2:17**), and even the restoration of all things promised to the Prophets (**Acts 3:20**). Re-digging the wells of Abraham is rediscovering the vision of the Apostles. As Isaac drank the waters that Abraham drank, we want to partake of the anointing that the Apostles walked in.

I was once asked on a national Israeli television program what our vision is as Messianic Jews. I answered that it was the same as all the prophets of Israel from Isaiah to Malachi: to establish the kingdom of God on earth, with peace among the nations, and the Messiah reigning from Jerusalem.

We have a spiritual inheritance from the Patriarchs, from the Prophets, and from the Apostles. That spiritual inheritance is available to all who will believe it and receive it—whether Jew or Gentile, man or woman, rich or poor.

SUPPLEMENT 12: GOSPEL OF THE KINGDOM

The gospel message starts with personal salvation through faith in Yeshua. This is the entry point of the kingdom of God for all human beings. Yet, the gospel of salvation is also referred to as the "gospel of the kingdom." Salvation continues on until its fullness in the kingdom of God.

Matthew 9:35 – preaching the gospel of the kingdom

Matthew 13:19 – the message of the kingdom

Matthew 24:14 – this gospel of the kingdom will be preached in all the world as a testimony to all the nations, and after that the end will come.

The kingdom is like a tiny mustard seed that eventually fills the earth (**Matthew 13:31-32**). Salvation is the planting of the seed; the kingdom is the process of it filling the earth (**Mark 4:26-29**). As all the elements of a tree are already present inside the seed, so has the Kingdom already come inside us. As the seed grows in stages to be a tree, so does the Kingdom grow until its fullness at Yeshua's return.

Let's try to give an outline of the wider kingdom gospel in the following 7 stages:

1. **Salvation** – receiving forgiveness of sins and eternal life through repentance and faith in the crucifixion and resurrection of Yeshua.

2. **Holy Spirit Baptism** – being filled with the power and presence of God, producing fruit of character and gifts of charisma in the life of the believer.

3. **Sanctified Life** – living as a dedicated disciple of Yeshua, including obedience to the Scriptures and the values of integrity and loyalty.

4. **Social Justice** – changing the world and society around us for better through the influence of godly values and spiritual power.

5. **Church and Israel** – working for the historic fullness, restoration and unity of both the Church and Israel leading up to the coming of Yeshua.

6. **Second Coming** – preparing the people of God to stand in the end times, declaring the soon coming of Yeshua in glory and judgment.

7. **Millennial Kingdom** – establishing the kingdom of the Messiah on earth with peace among the nations and Yeshua ruling from Jerusalem.

This understanding of the gospel as a presentation of all the dimensions of the kingdom of God, starting with repentance and salvation, yet ending up with Yeshua ruling and reigning on this planet, will have more and more significance as we approach Yeshua's return.

SUPPLEMENT 13: WALKING THROUGH ADVERSITY

By Phil Wagler

We are in a season of transition and tension, as we are being prepared for the coming of Jesus. When He comes, we will be like Him (**I John 3:2**). Therefore this is also a time of becoming more like Him. We will be then what we are becoming now.

He is bringing us into His likeness. He has ways of removing from us everything that is not like Him. His purposes are like a highway in our heart in which there are no obstacles or obstructions. We are to be fully available to Him.

Change happens by pressure. We stay the way we are until the pain of remaining the same becomes too great. God brings trials to pressure us into becoming complete (**James 1:2-4**). It is not enough to know an answer to a problem; we have to "walk it out." Walking through difficulties is the path to perfection.

Circumstances have no power over us. Every problem is an opportunity to be joyful. Faith is a decision to walk through circumstances which are beyond our abilities. We spend most of our time trying to get out of situations which God has prepared for us. We take the things we like and avoid what we do not like. We avoid adversity. Yet who we are is how we respond to adversity.

The issue is not what happens to us, but how we respond to it. The first priority is to fix our eyes on Yeshua (**Hebrews 12:1-3**). All sin is self-centered. We should look at life, not by asking, "How does this affect me?" but by asking "What is God trying to do?" Faith has a victory mentality, not a victim mentality.

God works through trials. We choose to be obedient (**Philippians 2:7**). Our faith is increased by walking through difficulties. The threat is in reverting to the old way of trying to do it in our own strength. Ask God to give you the grace to be empty and humble. Say, "I know you are God; I know you are good; I know you are in control."

God usually does not remove painful situations but gives us grace to go through them. That grace is our victory. Daniel was thrown in the lion's den and his friends into the fiery furnace. We must trust God's government over the circumstances in our life. The Church will be purified during the tribulation period. Tribulation is part of God's path to perfection. We will be like Him by the time He comes back.

SUPPLEMENT 14: HIGH AND LOW
by David Block

A tree can only grow as high as the depths of its roots allow it. Will we allow the Lord to get our roots deep by going way down and planting us where He so desires? You can only go as high as you have gone low. God desires to promote us. However, He often brings us to a low place before the promotion.

> **Psalm 75:6-7 – Not from the east nor from the west... come promotion and lifting up. God is the Judge! He puts down one and lifts up another.**

> **Job 5:11 – He sets on high those who are lowly, and those who mourn are lifted to safety.**

This is a spiritual principle: you can only be lifted to the degree that you have been brought low. This is why we humble ourselves before the Lord so that He can lift us up (**James 4:10**). We have to trust God to bring us into the low place and also to lift us up.

> **Luke 1:52 – He has put down the mighty from their thrones, and exalted the lowly.**

> **James 1:9 – Let the lowly brother glory in his exaltation.**

Yeshua is our teacher and Lord; He is the best example of being brought low and being lifted up. He shows us the way. Will we follow Him?

> **Matthew 21:5 – Behold, your King is coming to you, lowly and sitting on a donkey.**

Yeshua has taught us to be gentle and lowly of heart (Matthew 11:29). It is necessary to go to a lowly place; to be saturated there in order to become as He is before His plan can be allowed to be unfolded. Those low places mold us and make us who we are in Him. God is in the process of lifting us up, yet you can only go as high as you have gone low.

SUPPLEMENT 15: DON'T TOUCH THE BRIDE

Throughout the Scriptures the people of God are referred to as His bride. This metaphor starts in the Garden of Eden (**Genesis 2:18, 21-25**), through all the queens of Israel (especially Esther), the Song of Solomon, the wedding parables of the Gospel, Paul's epistles, the glorified woman (**Revelation 12**), the bride made ready (**Revelation 19:7**), and the marriage feast (**Revelation 19:9; 21:2, 9**). It is a great mystery (**Ephesians 5:32**).

In ancient times, those who took care of the wives of the king were eunuchs. They were given great delegated authority on the one obvious condition that they could not touch the affections of any of his brides.

We as dedicated followers of Yeshua are members of His spiritual bride. There are those of us who are called also to be "friends of the bridegroom" (**John 3:29**). They are part of the bride but also have some leadership to help prepare the bride for His coming. These co-leader-friends have special access to the people of God, to the heart of the bride. However, like spiritual eunuchs (**Matthew 19:12**), they must be sure not to steal the affections, attention, and ownership of the bride.

Those of us called to leadership must be very careful to die to the temptation of "stealing the attention" or "possessing the affections" of the people of God. We have the love and respect of the people but only to a secondary degree. This is true of worship leaders, pastors, preachers, and anyone in a place of authority or influence.

When we operate in the anointing of the Holy Spirit, people are drawn to us and to Yeshua in us. That is acceptable. At the Red Sea, the people of Israel believed in both God and Moses (**Exodus 14:31**). Yet Moses was very conscious not to pull the hearts of the people toward himself. (It took forty years in the desert to die to that tendency.)

The subconscious desire to gain affection and honor is incredibly dangerous and subtle. It lies at the root of the fall of Lucifer. May those of us in leadership enjoy the love and trust of the people of God, and we need to make sure that we never let the subtleties of pride lure us into "touching the bride." She is for Him.

SUPPLEMENT 16: APOSTOLIC MIRACLE BREAKTHROUGHS

The book of Acts holds a special place for all of us who are looking for the real "action" of the New Covenant apostles. We look to the first century community of disciples as our pattern of what faith should look like. This is a radical perspective on the book of Acts. "Acts" is not just a document of past actions, but a pattern for our present actions.

We want to preach the content of what they preached, live the lifestyle they lived, see the results they saw (and for us as Messianic Jews to relate to the Jewish community around us the way they did).

One element that stands out in the book of Acts is **supernatural miraculous intervention**. Just to look at a few examples, we see:

Acts 1:9 – Yeshua ascends into heaven before their eyes

Acts 2:3 – Tongues of fire fall on Shavuot morning

Acts 3:7 – Crippled man at the Temple mount instantly healed

Acts 4:31 – Earthquake during congregational prayer meeting

Acts 5:5 – Hananiah drops dead in prayer meeting after lying about money donated

Acts 5:19 – Angel opens the door to prison to set apostles free

Acts 6:15 – Stephen's face shines with glory light before the Sanhedrin

Acts 7:55 – Heavens open over Stephen's head as he is stoned

Acts 8:39 – Phillip is supernaturally transported from Gaza road to Ashdod

… And the list goes on throughout the book.

Another element we see is **growth in numbers of people saved**:

Acts 2:41 – 3,000 saved on Shavuot morning

Acts 2:47 – daily newly saved were being added

Acts 4:4 – 5,000 saved after crippled man healed

Acts 5:14 – more added despite persecution

Acts 6:1 – so many added that administrative problems arose between those who spoke Hebrew and those who spoke Greek

Acts 6:7 – numbers greatly increase in Jerusalem, including priests in Temple

Acts 8:6 – almost whole city of Samaria comes to faith by Phillip's ministry

Acts 11:21, 24 – many in Antioch come to Lord with Barnabas

Acts 16:5 – in cities throughout Greece numbers grew daily with Paul (Saul)

Acts 21:20 – 10's of thousands of religious Jews believe in Jerusalem with James (Yaakov)

… And the list goes on. The combination of supernatural power and evangelistic growth is part of what we are all praying for in a restoration of apostolic revival as in the book of Acts.

SUPPLEMENT 17: THREE STAGES OF BARNABAS

As there are people today fulfilling the roles of teacher, pastor, evangelist and prophet in the body of Messiah today, so are there those who are to fulfill the role of apostles (**Ephesians 4:11**). To argue that the apostles were only the original 12 in the first century would be parallel to saying that there were only 12 original teachers, pastors or evangelists, and none for today.

Apollos, Andronicus, Barnabas and others are all mentioned as apostles who were not among the original 12, or Paul the apostle himself (**Acts 14:14, Romans 16:7, I Corinthians 1:12**). In the case of Barnabas, there is enough description of his personal life to see how he developed into the function of apostolic ministry.

Barnabas (born in Cyprus of the tribe of Levi) is first mentioned as a dedicated young disciple in the early church. He had a gift of generosity and encouragement (**Acts 4:36-37**). He was both a "good" and "gifted" young man and soon was "sent out" by the apostles in Jerusalem to the church at Antioch. He encouraged others' faith and brought many to the Lord (**Acts 11:22-24**).

Here he began to function as a "missionary" (a semi-apostolic work) by being sent out to build up other churches, but he still did have the authority as an apostle. He had the gifting already but not yet the "office."

At Antioch he grew and ministered in the position of teacher and prophet (**Acts 13:1**). After prayer and fasting, the elders at Antioch perceived that the Holy Spirit was calling Paul and Barnabas into their own apostolic mission. They laid hands on them and sent them out (**Acts 13:3**). Now they were ordained as apostles but had not yet proven themselves.

After successfully spreading the kingdom of God and establishing congregations in a number of cities, Paul and Barnabas were recognized openly as apostles (**Acts 14:14**). At this point Barnabas was serving as a "co-apostle" with Paul.

Soon Barnabas had a different sense of direction from Paul and disagreed with him concerning discipline of the young John Mark (**Acts 15:37**). Here Barnabas decided to separate from Paul (**Acts 15:38**). It may be debated as to whether this was a wise decision or not; but in either case, we see Barnabas continuing on in his service to Cyprus in a separate sphere from Paul. (It is possible that Barnabas' authority as an apostle separate from Paul came into being as he returned to the country where he was born and raised.)

Barnabas' example shows how one who was not part of the original "12" can develop in his own faith and maturity into the role of an apostle.

SUPPLEMENT 18: RESTORATION OF ALL THINGS

There was a significant change in the apostles' understanding of the kingdom of God between Acts chapter one and chapter three - before and after the outpouring of the Holy Spirit.

Acts 1:6 – "Will You at this time restore the kingdom *to Israel*?"

Yeshua taught His disciples much about the kingdom of God after His resurrection (Acts 1:3). That vision was based in Israel and extended to the nations. Apparently the disciples heard the Israel part but missed the international part. That is why Yeshua told His disciples that they should be witnesses of Him **"from Jerusalem, Judea and Samaria, and to the ends of the earth"** – Acts 1:8.

The expansion in their thoughts was not only concerning people and places, but also time. They thought it all would take place right away, "at this time." However Yeshua told them that it was not for them to know the times or seasons (**Acts 1:7**). In retrospect, it has taken a much longer time than they expected for the message of the kingdom to get all the way around the world and back again to Israel.

When Simon Peter spoke a few weeks later in the Temple courtyards, he phrased his statement about the kingdom in a way which included the expansion of both time and quantity. **"…Messiah Yeshua, whom the heavens must receive until the time of the restoration of all things"** – Acts 3:20-21. He understood that Yeshua will not return until the spiritual foundations for the kingdom of God on the whole earth will be made ready.

Peter's view of the kingdom had enlarged not only from Israel to the nations, but to "all things" - including all things in creation, both in heaven and on earth (**Ephesians 1:10; Colossians 1:16**). The plan of the kingdom of God provides full restoration for everything spoken of in the Bible, both past and future.

Acts 3:21 gives a comprehensive definition of the kingdom of God: *the restoration of all things.* This was the vision of the early apostles. Let's make it ours as well.

SUPPLEMENT 19: INTEGRITY OF INDIGENOUS MINISTRY IN ISRAEL

In our generation we are witnessing the restoration of apostolic and prophetic ministry (**Ephesians 4:11-13**) in the body of Messiah worldwide. Little by little, apostolic and prophetic ministry is also being restored within the local remnant in Israel. Much of what is called apostolic or prophetic is inflated or phony. And much of what would be valid internationally is imported and not indigenous to Israel.

Paul spoke of powerful supernatural warfare in **II Corinthians 10:3-5**. The overall theme of chapters 10 – 12 is the battle to discern between true and false apostles (**II Corinthians 11:13**). Paul's primary spiritual warfare in these three chapters concerns the validity and integrity of apostolic ministry. What an eye-opening thought!

A great spiritual challenge before us and a deep passion of my heart is the *integrity of authentic, indigenous, apostolic authority in Israel*. To have authority, it must be authentic. To have integrity, it must be indigenous. A popular expression in Israeli is to produce "facts on the ground." Our spiritual version of this same saying would be to produce real fruit in real people here in the land of Israel.

[**Note:** Ministry has to be indigenous only to the degree that it calls itself "Israeli" or "Jewish." Otherwise it is not necessary. Indigenous elements include work experience, birthplace, family lineage, Hebrew language, taxes, cultural relevancy, historical perspective, current events, citizenship, army service, helping the needy and other types of practical service. Yeshua grew up and worked here 30 years before starting His teaching and evangelistic ministry.]

The restoration of apostolic-prophetic teams in Israel represents a partial restoration of the ministry of the original apostles of the first century. That restoration is a key element of right alignment and spiritual government for the greater body of Messiah.

If apostolic-prophetic ministry in Israel will have a humble and servant heart, it could be a source of blessing, revival, and unity. If it has integrity and authenticity, it could be an instrument of kingdom strategy as we prepare for the coming of Yeshua.

SUPPLEMENT 20: THE FIG TREE AND THE SECOND COMING

In Yeshua's primary teaching about the end times, He gave a parable about the fig tree. He said that the blossoming of the fig tree would be a sign that the Second Coming would be in that generation. Therefore, the fig tree parable has some "eschatological" significance

> **Matthew 24:32-34 – Learn this parable from the fig tree. When you see the branches growing soft and the leaves budding, know that the end is near... That generation will not pass away until all these things will happen.**

What is the fig tree? The fig tree is the nation of Israel. All the other nations of the world are also contained in the parable and are referred to as **"and all the trees"** – in the version in **Luke 21:29.** She has now come back to life after the two-thousand-year death of the exile.

What are the branches growing soft? That is the hearts of the people growing soft toward the possibility of faith in Yeshua. Toward the end of the year 2000, I began to notice a certain change in the heart of the people. Their hearts are softening. They are listening.

What are the leaves budding? That is the renewal of Jewish believers in Yeshua. At the time of this writing, there are over 100 Messianic fellowships in Israel. While most of them are small, they certainly would qualify as buds.

According to this interpretation of the parable, Yeshua may well return in the generation of the people alive here today.

SUPPLEMENT 21: SECOND PENTECOST

The holiday of Shavuot commemorates the beginning of the harvest season, the giving of the Law at Mount Sinai, and the outpouring of the Holy Spirit on Pentecost morning. The overlap of these three themes on the same day is a marvelous bit of biblical symbolism and prophetic meaning. Two thousand years ago, the early disciples of Yeshua were filled with the Holy Spirit and power.

Acts 2:1-4

When the day of Shavuot had fully come, they were all together in one accord in one place. And suddenly there came a sound from heaven, as of a rushing mighty wind, and it filled the whole house where they were sitting. Then there appeared to them divided tongues as of fire and rested upon each one of them. And they were all filled with the Holy Spirit and began to speak with other tongues as the Spirit gave them utterance.

This supernatural experience launched the gospel around the world and extended the kingdom of God to all nations. In explaining the experience to a gathering crowd, Simon Peter proclaimed that this was an initial fulfillment of a great end-times revival that would happen according to the prophecies of Joel. The same experience will happen again but to a much greater extent.

Acts 2:16-18, 21

This is that which was spoken of by the prophet Joel, "It will come to pass in the last days that I will pour out of My Spirit on all flesh, and your sons and daughters will prophesy; your young men will see visions, and your old men will dream dreams. And on my menservants and maidservants in those days, I will pour out My Spirit... And all who call upon the name of the Lord will be saved."

Peter was quoting the prophet Joel. Yet at the end he only quoted half a verse because the conditions were not ready for the second half of the prophecy. (This is similar to Yeshua's quoting the first part of Isaiah 61 in Luke 4 because the second part has to do with the Second Coming not the First.) Here is the other part of the verse in which Joel described the conditions for the "Second Pentecost."

Joel 2:32 – 3:2 ...because in Mount Zion and in Jerusalem there shall be a remnant, as the Lord has said, and among the survivors whom the Lord calls. Because behold in those days and at that

time as I will restore the captivity of Judah and Jerusalem, I will also gather all nations and bring them down to the valley of Yehoshphat; and there I will enter into judgment with them on account of My people, My heritage Israel...

Notice the word "because." The great outpouring will happen because of certain events having to do with a remnant in Mount Zion and Jerusalem.

Amazing! Two thousand years ago there was an initial outpouring of the Holy Spirit. That outpouring launched the gospel to the nations and is continuing today. As the gospel began to reach the ends of the world, God began to restore the nation of Israel and bring the Jews back to Jerusalem. We will be here for the events leading up to the Second Coming. As Israel was being restored, a great war broke out. Among the generation surviving World War II, God began to call many to believe in Yeshua.

Now a small remnant of Messianic Jews is in place in Israel. The events of the end times are close at hand. A horrible and larger World War will one day take place and, at the same time, a world-wide outpouring of the Holy Spirit. The Messianic remnant in Israel is a sign of the times and a spark of that revival. Let's pray the way the apostles did in the book of Acts and believe for the same results and even greater!

SUPPLEMENT 22: JOHN 17 AND ROMANS 11 UNITY

In John 17 Yeshua prays for the fullness of the international Church. This fullness includes union with God, unity among the believers in love, the glorification and sanctification by the Holy Spirit, and the final evangelizing of the world.

The John 17 prayer is connected to the parable of the Olive Tree in Romans 11. The various parts of the international Church are depicted as branches of different trees being grafted into one olive tree. The grafting causes unity because all the branches are grafted into the same tree. (For fuller description, see the chapter on John 17 - Romans 11 in our book *The Five Streams*)

God told Abraham that he was to be a "father of many nations" (**Genesis 17:4**). God's covenant with Abraham was that he was to adopt the spiritual children of all nations and to be a blessing to them. We as the Messianic remnant are called to walk in Abraham's footsteps by being a blessing to all our spiritual brothers and sisters who believe in Messiah Yeshua. In order to "adopt" other nations, we need to enlarge our hearts in love (**II Corinthians 6:12, 7:2**).

The international *Ecclesia* may be seen as a family of families. The remnant of Israel is supposed to be the *elder brother* of the family. The role of the *elder brother* or *first born son* is to unify the extended family. As Messianic Jews embrace the prayer of John 17 for unity, the international Church will embrace its grafting in to the Romans 11 tree. We all have to develop a heart to serve and support one another. Then together we can advance Yeshua's kingdom.

SUPPLEMENT 23: THE TWO STICKS PROPHECY

In **Ezekiel 37:15-23** the prophet is instructed to take two sticks and write on one, "For Judah and the sons of Israel, his companions" and on the other, "For Joseph, the stick of Ephraim and the whole house of Israel." Then he is to join the two sticks in his hand, which symbolizes the healing of the separation between the two. This parable originated in the split between the sons of Leah (Judah) and Rachel (Joseph); then in the generation after Solomon, the entire kingdom was divided, the southern one called "Judah" and the northern one "Israel."

There are many spiritual applications of this prophecy. For example, in 1948 the modern state was named Israel, not Judah. Secular Israelis tend to use the name "Israel," whereas the religious tend to use the name "Jew" or "Judah". The Prime Minister often struggles to bring unity between secular and religious; left wing and right.

The Hebrew for "stick" in this passage is עץ "ets", which is the same word for "wood" or "tree." The passage could also be understood as bringing "two trees into one." This provides a background for Paul's description in Romans 11 of different types of branches being grafted into one olive tree.

The Judah stick contained the "sons of Israel," while the Joseph stick included the "whole house of Israel." This extended "house of Israel" may also be the context for Paul's statement in **Ephesians 2:12** that Gentile believers from all the nations become part of the greater "commonwealth of Israel." (In other words, it is possible to be part of the greater "spiritual" house of Israel by faith in Yeshua, without being born of Israelite physical lineage.)

The parable indicates God's desire for unity among His people. It was Ezekiel's job as prophet to intercede on behalf of that unity. There is an ongoing spiritual battle in which evil forces try to divide the kingdom of God (**Luke 11:17**). Godly people in every generation find themselves standing in the gap between two groups, holding on to one in the right hand and one in the left.

The Two Sticks is an essential link in the series of end-times prophecies including the Dry Bones (**Ezekiel 37**), Gog and Magog (**Ezekiel 38-39**) and the Messianic Kingdom (**Ezekiel 40-48**). The intercession to hold on to seemingly contradictory dimensions of the kingdom of God requires effort and perseverance in the face of much opposition. Let us grasp the two sticks in our hands as we pray according to the spirit as Ezekiel did.

SUPPLEMENT 24: MILLENNIAL AUTHORITY

By Solomon Intrater

Jesus said to Peter, "I will give you the keys of the kingdom of heaven; whatever you bind on earth will be bound in heaven and whatever you loose on earth will be loosed in heaven" (**Matthew 16:19**). There have been different interpretations and implications to this passage. Did Jesus intend to delegate authority to Peter to administrate a new institution? Could the meaning of this be *halakhic*, to be the authority on Jewish law? Or was this about spiritual power to heal the sick and cast out demons?

Institutional Tradition

It is said that nothing begins without the (innovative) action of men; yet nothing (concrete) lasts without building institutions. This brings to mind the apologetic argument for orthodox traditional authority in Christianity as well as in Judaism. Can generational authority be delegated through institutions? This is logic found at the beginning of *Pirkei Avot*, that at first there was Moses and he delegated authority to Joshua, all the way through biblical prophets and scribes to proto-Rabbinic figures like Hillel and then Yochanan Ben-Zakai. With this argument, ordained Rabbis today in Orthodox Judaism are considered authoritative, because the institution, the traditional authority, is revered.

This is the same logic of the traditional institutional Church, particularly in Roman Catholicism. Jesus ordained Peter, and that ordination was passed on from Pope to Pope. The institution itself is consecrated. In this sense of authority, *messianism* is inclined to be at odds with traditional institutions. With an apocalyptic sense of urgency, messianic figures and their agents, with bold proclamations and movements, are inclined to *revolutionize* institutional systems of authority.

It is difficult to think that Jesus had a traditional institution in mind even when he spoke to Peter about *ecclesia*. Likewise, it is problematic when people and movements outside of traditional institutions separate themselves from the system, and then also call for a new chain of generational leadership.

It would generally make more sense for activists to reform the existing institutions, instead of simply beginning a new institutional tradition. Of course, if the end is near, then this is an altogether different scenario. If the world is about to be transformed, then it is timely to be a messianic revolutionary, but there is also no need for a new form of tradition, because all things will be transformed.

Charismatic Leadership

Paul wrote in **Romans 13:1-5** that appointed leadership is under the supervision of God. The book of **Daniel** in the Bible emphasizes the common biblical theme that *God* is sovereign, whereas mighty empires rise and fall. But the way we treat people in minor positions of authority in everyday life might be a slightly different issue to tackle from these lofty statements, especially for the "Millennial Generation" (a term referring loosely to the younger generation growing up after the year 2000 in the midst of massive changes in technology and information systems).

The world is becoming more and more flat. That means, not only are we exposed to a global community, but also that the traditional role of authority seems to be leveling out. In the past, societies were administered by an elite class while the masses were uneducated and underprivileged. So naturally, authority was revered, and there was a stark contrast between officers and underlings. But that gap becomes generally more narrow in modern democratic society where equal rights and education are available to all. If knowledge is power, then knowledge and power are less esoteric than the past. This has created an historically unprecedented cultural exchange.

Authority and leadership are not the same thing, although ideally they would come together. Leadership is subjective, it involves inspiration and affirmation. In other words, *charisma*. But such charisma is rather independent of authority. People cannot place their hopes in every employer and politician. There is such a thing as a professional relationship! Millennials do not necessarily have less esteem for authority itself, but are generally skeptical in regards to the *charismatic leadership* of an authority until proven otherwise.

When people invest their hopes in authority and leadership only to be disappointed, this generates a serious problem. The nature of a child is normally to trust, naively; whereas rebellion is often an acquired trait; a *reaction*. Young people today are desperate for affirmation, for inspiration and for faith. While exemplary behavior and affirmation are always desirable and positive, they are only *necessary* in a few cases, such as for a child to a father, for a soldier to a captain, and to God.

If charisma is automatically attributed to authority, than we are led back to the institutional traditional logic. However, there is a distinction between institutional authority and charismatic leadership. You can give someone a position of authority, but you cannot make them charismatic leaders. With position comes authority, but genuine charisma is a dynamic which can only be built *directly* between "leader" and assembly.

The vision and ideals that lead us are greater than the men and women, flesh and blood, or *institutions* that temporarily embody them. The messianic authority of Jesus was non-institutional yet powerfully charismatic. His declaration of *Kingdom* was prophetic, mysterious and full of zeal. May God grant us mercy and bless us with zeal, amen.

Asher and Betty Intrater serve on the senior leadership teams at Ahavat Yeshua Congregation in Jerusalem, Tiferet Yeshua Congregation in Tel Aviv, Revive Israel Ministries, and Tikkun International. Asher is also one of the founding board members of the Messianic Jewish Alliance of Israel. He holds degrees from Harvard University, Baltimore Hebrew College and Messiah Biblical Institute. Asher has authored *Covenant Relationships, The Apple of His Eye, The Five Streams, Iraq to Armageddon, What does the Bible Really Say about the Land?, Who Ate Lunch with Abraham?* and *Israel, the Church and the Last Days* (co-authored with Dan Juster). Revive Israel's weekly e-mail teaching and prayer update is currently being translated into 14 different languages.

For more information, and to receive ministry updates, please visit

WWW.REVIVEISRAEL.ORG

Advancing the kingdom of God as an Israeli-based apostolic ministry team

Revive Israel is a multi-purpose ministry team, based on the model of Yeshua with His twelve in the Gospels and Paul and his ministry team in the book of Acts. Our team functions as a "fivefold" or "apostolic" ministry, each member being trained for the full release of his gifts and callings.

The vision of Revive Israel is to foster revival in the land of Israel and the Nations. We believe in the simple and direct sharing of the gospel, training disciples, and building up congregations in Israel and around the world.

Please join with us in prayer and teaching each week by subscribing to our email updates.

Visit us at

www.reviveisrael.org

and sign-up today.

**A network of emissaries in Israel and around the world
working toward the restoration of Israel and the unity of
Jew and Gentile in the Body of Messiah.**

The Tikkun International mission is to effectively fulfill Yeshua's (Jesus') Great Commission through an apostolic network that restores the synergy of five-fold leadership to provide effective accountability and oversight to leaders, ministries and congregations through covenant relationships and mutual support.

Tikkun International fulfills its mission by:

1. Equipping, educating and sending forth those called to Messianic Jewish ministry from the Diaspora.

2. Fundraising, charitable aide and support for aliyah to Israel and for indigenous international ministries.

3. Empowering a network of Messianic Jewish Congregations through biblical governance and partnerships in education, training, national conferences, and leadership development.

4. Exhorting and educating the Church regarding her Jewish roots and responsibilities to the Jewish people.

5. Partnering with Church leaders for the full restoration of Israel and the Church.

Please visit Tikkun International at
www.tikkunministries.org

Planting Congregations and Giving to the Needy in Israel

Our vision is to be an oasis for Israel's returning exiles and for her native-born sons and daughters. In the ancient Near East the oasis was an absolutely vital center of refuge, supply, healing, equipping and sending out. This vision is being fulfilled as:

- A HUMANITARIAN AID CENTER, providing practical assistance to new immigrants, operating out of an industrial warehouse.

- A SHARING COMMUNITY MEETING IN HOUSE GROUPS, which seek the healing and equipping of each member for the work of the Lord.

- A MESSIANIC SYNAGOGUE CELEBRATING THE TORAH ROOTS of our New Covenant faith, embracing Jesus as Israel's Messiah, declaring Yeshua, Come Home!!!

- A TABERNACLE OF PRIESTLY WORSHIP AND INTERCESSION where God's presence is sought passionately.

- A CONGREGATION PLANTING CENTER, in the apostolic pattern of extending God's Kingdom through sending out teams to do humanitarian aid, evangelism and congregation planting in unreached areas of Israel.

Please visit Tents of Mercy at
www.tentsofmercy.org

Yad Hashmona is a small moshav in central Israel, located in the Judean Mountains near Jerusalem, within the jurisdiction of Mateh Yehuda Regional Council.

Yad Hashmona was founded in 1971 by a small group of Finnish Christians. It is named for eight Jewish refugees from Austria who escaped to Finland in 1938. The Finnish government, collaborating with the Nazis, handed the refugees over to the Gestapo in 1942. Seven of them died in Auschwitz. In 1978, a group of messianic Jews joined the moshav. Most of the members are now Israelis and the main spoken language is Hebrew. Due to intermarriage with Israeli Jews the moshav has become a center of Messianic Jews in Israel.

The Moshav boasts a hotel, restaurant, and Biblical garden and is a local attraction for visitors to Israel from around the world.

Please visit Yad Hashmona at
www.yad8.com

WILBUR
MINISTRIES

Paul Wilbur is an Integrity Music recording artist and the founder of Wilbur Ministries.

Paul and his team travel throughout the United States and the world sharing the love of God through Yeshua (Jesus) the Messiah. In 1990 Paul recorded his first release with Integrity entitled "Up To Zion." Since then he has recorded five more solo albums including three performed live in Jerusalem: "Shalom Jerusalem," "Jerusalem Arise," and "Lion Of Judah." "Holy Fire" (1997) and "The Watchman" (2006) were recorded in Houston and San Antonio respectively. Two more special release collections entitled "Pray For The Peace of Jerusalem" and "Praise Adonai" were released in 2007 and 2008 to honor the 60th birthday of Israel and the 40th anniversary of the re-unification of Jerusalem.

Paul has also recorded seven projects in Spanish and two in Portuguese. These award-winning discs enable the team to minister to more than one third of the world's population in their own language!

Wilbur Ministries is headquartered in Jacksonville, Florida, where Paul makes his home with his wife Luanne. Their two sons Nathan, his wife Malki and Joel, and his wife Sharon Chernoff Wilbur also live in the area and play important roles in the life of the ministry.

Please visit Wilbur Ministries at
www.wilburministries.com

Al Hayat TV

Alhayat TV also known as *Life TV* is an Arabic television channel, which airs to viewers in countries in North Africa, West Asia, the Middle East, America, Canada, Australia and some of Europe.

It began airing in September 2003, largely from Egypt, Alhayat is evangelical in its aims, and explains in its Website Mission Statement that "Jesus Christ came to earth to destroy the works of the devil and his blood shed on the cross to redeem humanity and restore the broken relationship with God to come back."

It can be viewed live from its official website :
www.hayatv.tv

עָרוּץ הַחֲדָשׁוֹת הַטּוֹבוֹת

YESHUA CHAI TV

A Hebrew Internet TV Channel declaring that Yeshua is the way, the truth and the Life

Launched in 2012, Yeshua Chai TV is a Internet-based broadcast that tells the stories of Israeli Messianic Jews from all walks of life.

This innovative outreach project hopes to demonstrate that Israeli, Jewish followers of Yeshua are nothing but regular Israelis following the Jewish Messiah Yeshua.

Please visit Yeshua Chai TV at
www.yeshuachai.tv

JERUSALEM
INSTITUTE OF JUSTICE
CORPORATION FOR THE BENEFIT OF THE PUBLIC

The Jerusalem Institute of Justice is dedicated to cultivating and defending the rule of law, human rights, freedom of conscience and democracy for all people in Israel and its adjacent territories.

Within Israel, we pursue freedom of religion, freedom of conscience, and advocate for members of minority religions, as well as citizens lacking any religious affiliation. We have also done extensive work on behalf of victims of human trafficking, advanced affirmative action for Ethiopian new immigrants, and provided representation to Lone Soldiers who have been abandoned by their ultra-Orthodox families for choosing to serve in the IDF.

Our passion for freedom, truth and moral clarity has driven us to pursue justice, not only within Israel, but also on behalf of Israel. While most human rights organizations superficially point to Israel's occupation of the disputed territories as the foremost abuse of human rights in our region, we espouse a more thorough and balanced view on the matter. We have drafted and disseminated extensive reports on the human rights abuses of the Palestinian Authority (PA) in the West Bank and the Hamas government in Gaza.

Please visit JIJ at
www.jij.org.il

Maoz Israel Ministries, a Messianic Jewish ministry in Israel, is a catalyst & vehicle for outreach, training, translating, publishing, music recording, video production, economic and disaster relief, and has established and underwrites an indigenous, Hebrew-speaking Messianic Jewish congregation in Tel Aviv.

Our ultimate goal is to see the Israeli people accept the atonement of their Messiah Yeshua as promised in Scripture.

While we continue to reach out to our people, we also have more specific goals:

1. To teach the Bible - the Old and New Covenants - as the basis to know the way to abundant life in this world and eternal life in the next.
2. Establish a safe environment which will allow fellowship for Messianic believers, a steady personal spiritual growth for new believers and be a vehicle for outreach throughout Israel.
3. Help Israeli believers mature in their faith and personal walk with the Lord.
4. Financially help the poor and needy believers in Israel, as well as victims of war and terror.
5. Help Israeli believers persecuted for their faith in Messiah as they fight for freedom of religion.
6. Help new immigrant believers and young Israeli believers, who are the future of the Messianic Movement in Israel, reach their full potential.

Outside Israel, our goal is to spread awareness among the nations of the world about Israel and the Middle East conflict, and give a prophetic perspective for current events in Israel.

Please visit Maoz Israel at
www.maozisrael.org

Gateways Beyond International is a Messianic missional community committed to sharing a life of daily worship and prayer, discipleship training and world outreach.

Gateways Beyond has a vision to train, equip, and launch young Messianic believers into world outreach. Our intensive six-month training school offers classroom study and practical experience, specifically for those believers with a clear call to Jewish world outreach. Areas of concentration include: intimacy with God, character building discipleship, worship & intercession, servanthood and Jewish outreach. Each school will culminate in a 4-6 week outreach, applying the classroom training to real life ministry.

Currently, Gateways Schools exist in Cyprus, Switzerland, and Washington State.

Please visit Gateways Beyond at
www.gatewaysbeyond.org

Equipping God's people with His heart and purpose for Israel and the nations.

Caleb Company's name was inspired by Israel's fearless warrior, Caleb, who along with Joshua, brought a good report concerning the land of Israel in the midst of great opposition.

Our non-profit ministry was founded by Dr. Don Finto in 1996. As a pastor to pastors, Don "fathers" leaders in Israel and the nations. He is an international speaker and author of two best-selling books concerning God's heart and end-time plan for Israel and the nations.

After serving in leadership with Youth With A Mission for fourteen years, Tod McDowell relocated his family to Nashville, Tennessee in 2007 to work full-time with Caleb Company. In 2010, Don shifted his role to serve as Caleb's President and Tod became Executive Director. During this transitional season, we have grown into a thriving local community with a team of staff, interns, and alumni focused on fulfilling the Caleb vision.

Please visit Caleb Company at
www.calebcompany.org

Aglow International is a Kingdom Movement committed to seeing God's will done on earth as it is in Heaven.

Aglow International is a Kingdom community of more than 200,000 warriors, champions, and global leaders who touch 17 million people annually.

As a Kingdom Movement, Aglow's ultimate goal is to see every nation touched and every heart changed. Aglow has established powerful Kingdom communities founded on the fullness of Christ, in over 170 nations.

We are committed to seeing God's will done on earth as it is in Heaven by raising up individuals who will bring freedom to the oppressed, while providing opportunities for everyone in our spheres of influence to grow into radiant relationships with the Father, Son, and Holy Spirit, as well as, with each other.

Visit Aglow International at
www.aglowinternational.org

INTERNATIONAL
HOUSE *of* PRAYER

The Lord has called us to be a community of believers committed to God, each other, and to establishing and maintaining a 24/7 house of prayer in Kansas City—a perpetual solemn assembly gathering corporately to fast and pray, in the spirit of the tabernacle of David.

On May 7, 1999, the International House of Prayer of Kansas City (IHOPKC) was founded by Mike Bickle and twenty full-time "intercessory missionaries," who cried out to God in prayer with worship for thirteen hours each day. Four months later, on September 19, 1999, prayer and worship extended to the full 24/7 schedule.

The International House of Prayer is an evangelical missions organization that is committed to praying for the release of the fullness of God's power and purpose, as we actively win the lost, heal the sick, feed the poor, make disciples, and impact every sphere of society—family, education, government, economy, arts, media, religion, etc. Our vision is to work in relationship with the wider Body of Christ to engage in the Great Commission, as we seek to walk out the two great commandments to love God and people.

Please visit IHOP-KC at
www.ihopkc.org